MENTAL MODELS
for MATH

Grades 6–12

Mental Models for Math Grades 6–12
206 pp.

ISBN-13: 978-1-929229-53-6
ISBN-10: 1-929229-53-4

1. Education   2. Sociology   3. Title

Contributors Bethanie H. Tucker, Ed.D. and Shelley Rex conceptualized and designed many of the mental models. Special thanks to the other consultants from **aha!** Process, Inc. who also participated in the effort. For specifics regarding credits, see pp. 205–206.

Copy editing by Dan Shenk
Book design by Paula Nicolella
Cover design by ArtLink, Inc.

MENTAL MODELS
for MATH

Grades 6–12

FOREWORD

The theory of mental models was first introduced by Kenneth Craik, a British philosopher and psychologist, in his 1943 book *The Nature of Explanation*. After his untimely death in a bicycle accident in 1945 (at age 31), the idea did not re-emerge in the literature until 1983 with the publication of Philip Johnson-Laird's book *Mental Models*.

Mental models have been defined as internalized, mental representations of things in the world—or internal symbols or representations of external phenomena. The representation that a person develops determines how he/she understands and interacts with the world. The more accurate the mental model, the more successful the interaction.

Mental models are believed to play a major part in cognition. When learners develop a more complete, accurate, and richer model of a particular domain, they become more competent in that domain. A teacher's main responsibility is to mediate students' learning so they formulate accurate, complete mental representations of abstract concepts as efficiently as possible.

The term *mental model*, as used in the field of education and in this workbook, is intended to describe strategies, visual representations, analogies, and stories that assist in the development of accurate internal symbols. Each mental model is designed to move the student closer to a deeper and richer understanding of the standards and abstract concepts necessary for success in the academic setting, as well as meaningful interaction with the world.

TABLE OF CONTENTS

Please note that the symbol appears in the top corner of the page at the beginning of each individual lesson series. Each lesson consists of a mental model for the standard, a step sheet for the student and teacher, and an assessment rubric.

INTRODUCTION

Mental Models for Math

This workbook contains examples of mental models that teachers in middle school through high school can use in explaining mathematical concepts.

The following information, taken from *Understanding Learning: the How, the Why, the What* by Dr. Ruby K. Payne, explains the characteristics and purposes of mental models.

- Mental models are how the mind holds abstract information, i.e., information that has no sensory representation.

- All subject areas or disciplines have their own blueprint or mental models.

- Mental models tell us what is and is not important in the discipline. They help the mind to sort.

- Mental models often explain the "why" of things working the way they do.

- Mental models tell the structure, purpose, or pattern of the discipline.

- Mental models are held in the mind as stories, analogies, movements, or two-dimensional drawings.

- Mental models "collapse" the amount of time it takes to teach/learn something.

- Mental models of a discipline are contained within the curriculum.

Mathematics, for example is about assigning order and value to the universe.

The mental models in this workbook involve four types: Pictures, Movement, Stories, and Analogies. All can be used effectively by teachers.

I. Pictorial Mental Models

Pythagorean Theorem: $a^2 + b^2 = c^2$

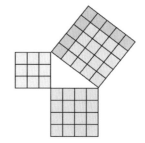

$$a^2 + b^2 = c^2$$
$$3^2 + 4^2 = 5^2$$
$$9 + 16 = 25$$
$$25 = 25$$

Many of the mental models contained in this workbook are two-dimensional drawings of three-dimensional concepts. The above drawing is a mental model that explains the Pythagorean Theorem. It is a two-dimensional representation of an abstract concept. This mental model is effective because it enables the reader to grasp the concept and the instructor to explain it in less time than would be required through oral instructions alone.

II. Movement Mental Models

An example of a movement mental model in mathematics is where students use a smile and frown to identify right-side-up and upside-down parabolas. If the parabola opens up, the leading coefficient is positive and matches the smile.
If the parabola opens down, the leading coefficient is negative and matches the frown. A movement mental model reflects a concept, generalization, or discipline.

Parabolas
Graphing Quadratic Functions:
The Leading Coefficient

Designed by Shelley Rex

III. Story Mental Models

Story mental models can range from cartoons that explain one concept or vocabulary word to chapter books that illustrate many related and interrelated concepts and generalizations. Several of the mental models in this workbook follow the story format, specifically that of cartoons.

IV. Analogy Mental Models

An example of an analogy mental model is the use of "Gallon Guy" to teach liquid measurement. In this mental model, arms and legs are to the trunk of the body as quarts are to a gallon.

Designed by Kim Ellis

NOTE: Many mental models are a combination of two or more types.

Mental models tell the structure, purpose, or patterns of the discipline

As noted, math is about assigning order and value to the universe. We tend to assign order and value in three ways: numbers, space, and/or time.

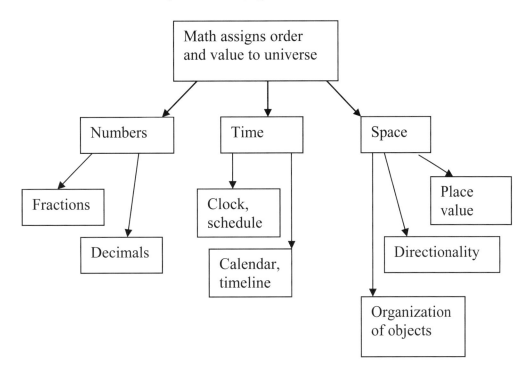

Mental Models—the Ultimate Goal

The ultimate goal when working with mental models is for students to develop their own effective, personal mental models. Here is a step sheet to guide students in their progress.

Step Sheet for Student Development of Mental Models

1. Highlight or write out the concept for which you will develop a mental model.

2. Decide which type of mental model would be most effective for explaining the concept: pictorial, movement, story, analogy.

3. Take your time to develop your mental model in your mind.

4. Sketch, draw, or explain in a story your mental model.

5. Assess each component for efficiency, accuracy, and clarity.

6. Revise your mental model as your understanding of the concept grows.

CHAPTER ONE
Numbers and Operations

Most numbers can be written as fractions:

$$\frac{1}{8} \qquad \frac{8}{1} = 8 \qquad \frac{10987819279387512893 8}{91829301237158972385 7}$$

Their *ratios* can be named.

If their *ratios* can be named, they must be

rational numbers.

Some numbers cannot be written as fractions:

2.95783991 … $\sqrt{2} = 1.414213 …$

Their *ratios* cannot be named.

They must be

irrational numbers.

Example: $\sqrt{2}$ ("Square root of 2") is not rational. There is no whole number, fraction, or decimal whose square is 2.

www.ahaprocess.com

MENTAL MODEL—NUMBERS AND OPERATIONS

Standard: Numbers and Operations

Understand numbers, ways of representing numbers, relationships among numbers, and number systems.

Compare and contrast the properties of numbers and number systems, including the rational and real numbers.

Explanation of Mental Model:

This "poster style" mental model is designed for frequent viewing.

STEP SHEET

1. Read the mental model.
2. Examine the relationship between the words *ratio* and *fraction*. (Ratios can be written as fractions.)
3. Compare the words ratio and rational. Numbers that can be written as a ratio (fractions) are rational.
4. Write definitions of the following terms in your own words: ratio, fraction, rational number, and irrational number.
5. Design your own mental model that explains rational and irrational numbers.

RUBRIC

Standard: Numbers and Operations

Understand numbers, ways of representing numbers, relationships among numbers, and number systems.

Compare and contrast the properties of numbers and number systems, including the rational and real numbers.

Criteria	4 Exceeds Standard	3 Meets Standard	2 Is Below Standard	1 Does Not Meet Standard
Relationships among numbers	Can give real-life examples of ratios, fractions, and rational and irrational numbers	Can compare, contrast, and define ratios, fractions, and rational and irrational numbers	Can compare, contrast, and define three of four terms: ratios, fractions, and rational and irrational numbers	Can compare, contrast, or define fewer than three of terms
Mental model	Develops mental model that could be used as example for classroom	Develops accurate and adequate personal mental model	Develops mental model that encompasses portion of concepts	Cannot develop mental model that explains concepts
Process	Can explain relationship between ratios and fractions	Can read ratios as fractions	Needs minimal assistance in reading ratios as fractions	Cannot read ratios as fractions with minimal assistance

www.ahaprocess.com

Practice for Mental Math

1	3	5	7
9	11	13	15
17	19	21	23
25	27	29	

2	3	6	7
10	11	14	15
18	19	22	23
26	27	30	

4	5	6	7
12	13	14	15
20	21	22	23
28	29	30	

8	9	10	11
12	13	14	15
24	25	26	27
28	29	30	

16	17	18	19
20	21	22	23
24	25	26	27
28	29	30	

MENTAL MODEL—NUMBERS AND OPERATIONS

Standard: Numbers and Operations

Compute fluently and make reasonable estimates.

Explanation of Mental Model:

This mental model is an enjoyable math game that relies on fluent mental computation, preparing the student for mental math.

STEP SHEET

Preparations: Reproduce the Mental Math Magic Cards and cut them apart.

I. Mental Math Magic Show

1. Ask a friend to think of a number between 1 and 30. He/she should not tell you the number.
2. Show the student the first Mental Math card and ask him/her if the number chosen is on that card.
3. If he/she says, "No," do nothing.
4. If he/she says, "Yes," make a mental note of the first number on the card (in the upper-left corner).
5. Repeat with the second card, then the third, etc.
6. Add the numbers from the upper-left corner of all the cards to which your friend responds, "Yes."
7. The total of the numbers that you add in your head (the cards for which your friend said, "Yes") will equal the chosen number.

II. Magic of Your Own

1. Examine the cards to determine why this game works.
2. Put the Mental Math Magic Cards away and reconstruct them on your own, using mathematical logic.
3. Compare your cards with the originals.

RUBRIC

Standard: Numbers and Operations

Compute fluently and make reasonable estimates.

Criteria	4 Exceeds Standard	3 Meets Standard	2 Is Below Standard	1 Does Not Meet Standard
Process	Can design new mental math game	Can explain concept behind math cards	Approximates concept behind math cards	Cannot explain concept behind math cards
Computation (fluency)	Can play game quickly and with no errors	Can play game with few errors	Can play game slowly or with some errors	Cannot play game successfully
Problem solving	Reproduces cards accurately and effortlessly	Reproduces cards with some effort	Reproduces cards with minimal assistance	Cannot reproduce cards with minimal assistance
Mathematical language	Uses precise and accurate mathematical terms when explaining concept of game	Gives accurate explanation of game	Explains the game with minimal assistance	Cannot accurately explain game with minimal assistance

 = infinity symbol

MENTAL MODEL—NUMBERS AND OPERATIONS

Standard: Numbers and Operations

Understand numbers, ways of representing numbers, relationships among numbers, and number systems.

Explanation of Mental Model:

This "poster style" mental model is designed for frequent viewing.

STEP SHEET

1. Read the mental model.
2. Write your own definition of *infinity*.
3. Research the symbol for infinity.
4. Design your own mental model for the symbol for or the concept of infinity.

RUBRIC

Standard: Numbers and Operations

Understand numbers, ways of representing numbers, relationships among numbers, and number systems.

Criteria	4 Exceeds Standard	3 Meets Standard	2 Is Below Standard	1 Does Not Meet Standard
Mental model	Designs mental model that could be used as example for classroom	Designs appropriate personal mental model	Designs mental model that approximates concept	Cannot design appropriate mental model
Problem solving	Identifies possible use of infinity symbol in environment	Uses infinity symbol accurately in math class	Uses infinity symbol with few errors	Frequently misuses infinity symbol in mathematical context
Mathematical language	Refers to infinity symbol accurately outside classwork to communicate mathematically	Refers to infinity symbol accurately in classwork	Refers to infinity symbol with few errors	Cannot accurately describe or refer to infinity symbol

     www.ahaprocess.com

Place Value

This is a money machine. It spits out one-dollar bills. My job is to stand here in the ones column and collect the bills. When I get ten of them I wrap them together and pass them on to the man in the tens column.

Right now I have $3.

I have six stacks of ones. That's sixty ones in all.

When I collect ten stacks of ones I have $100. I wrap them up and pass them on to the lady in the hundreds column.

I have four stacks of hundreds.

When I collect ten stacks of hundreds I bundle them up and pass them on to the man in the thousands column.

I have three stacks of thousands. That's $3,000.

The process continues into the ten thousands, hundred thousands, millions columns, and so on.

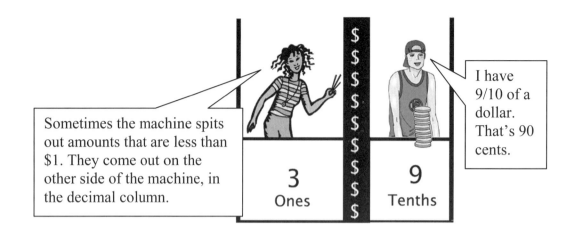

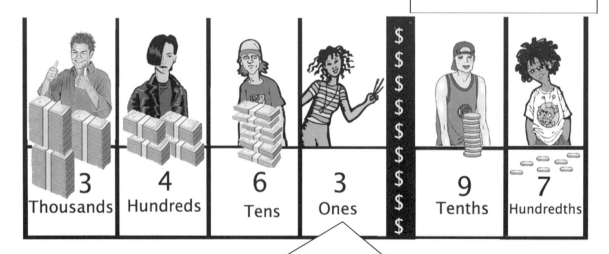

www.ahaprocess.com

MENTAL MODEL—NUMBERS AND OPERATIONS

Standard: Numbers and Operations

Understand numbers, ways of representing numbers, relationships among numbers, and number systems.

Understand the place-value structure of the base-10 number system and be able to represent and compare whole numbers and decimals.

Explanation of Mental Model:

This mental model is designed to provide a concrete explanation of the abstract concept of place value.

STEP SHEET

1. Examine the place value mental model.
2. Write a paragraph explaining place value in your own words.
3. Make a list of at least 10 situations that would require numbers less than 1.
4. Design a mental model of your own that illustrates place value, decimal points, and decimal columns showing "less than 1."

RUBRIC

Standard: Numbers and Operations

Understand numbers, ways of representing numbers, relationships among numbers, and number systems.

	4	3	2	1
Criteria	**Exceeds Standard**	**Meets Standard**	**Is Below Standard**	**Does Not Meet Standard**
Mental model	Designs mental model that could be used as example for classroom	Designs accurate personal mental model	Designs mental model illustrating place value that approximates concepts	Cannot design mental model that illustrates concepts
Mathematical language (1)	Can list numerous situations that would call for less than 1	Can list five situations that would call for less than 1	Can list fewer than five situations that would call for less than 1	Cannot list more than one situation that would call for less than 1
Mathematical language (2)	Writes a paragraph explaining place value that could be used to as example for classroom	Writes an accurate paragraph explaining place value	Writes paragraph with minimal assistance	Cannot write accurate paragraph explaining place value with minimal assistance

Rounding

About how many <u>ones</u> do you have?

$3,463.90 is between three thousand four hundred sixty-three and three thousand four hundred sixty-four. $3,463.90 is closer to $3,464 than it is to $3,463, so I'll round up.

I have about three thousand four hundred sixty-four dollars.

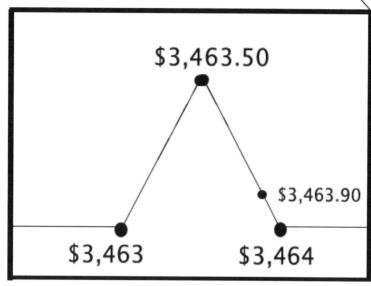

$3,463.90 is between three thousand four hundred sixty and three thousand four hundred seventy. $3,463.90 is closer to $3,460 than it is to $3,470, so I'll round down.

I have about three thousand four hundred sixty dollars.

About how many <u>tens</u> do you have?

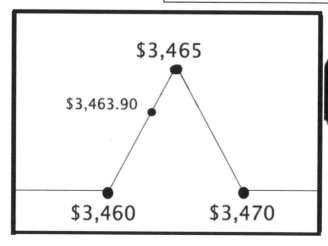

About how many <u>hundreds</u> do you have?

$3,463.90 is between three thousand four hundred and three thousand five hundred. $3,463.90 is closer to $3,500 than it is to $3,400, so I'll round up.

I have about three thousand five hundred dollars.

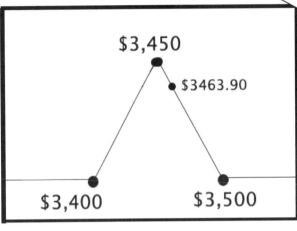

About how many <u>thousand</u> dollars do you have?

$3,463.90 is between three thousand and four thousand. $3,463.90 is closer to $3,000 than it is to $4,000, so I'll round down.

I have about three thousand dollars.

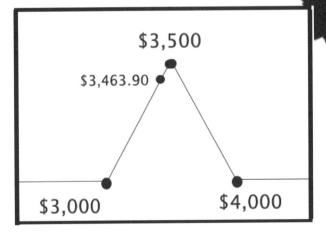

MENTAL MODEL—NUMBERS AND OPERATIONS

Standard: Numbers and Operations

Understand numbers, ways of representing numbers, relationships among numbers, and number systems.

Understand the place-value structure of the base-10 number system and be able to represent and compare whole numbers and decimals.

Explanation of Mental Model:

This mental model is designed to provide a concrete explanation of the abstract concept of rounding off.

STEP SHEET

1. Examine the mental model.
2. Write a paragraph explaining "rounding" numbers in your own words.
3. List five situations in which an exact number is not needed or preferred.
4. Design a personal mental model that illustrates "rounding."

RUBRIC

Standard: Numbers and Operations

Understand numbers, ways of representing numbers, relationships among numbers, and number systems.

Understand the place-value structure of the base-10 number system and be able to represent and compare whole numbers and decimals.

Criteria	4 Exceeds Standard	3 Meets Standard	2 Is Below Standard	1 Does Not Meet Standard
Mental model	Designs mental model for rounding that could be used as example for classroom	Designs appropriate personal mental model for rounding	Designs mental model for rounding that approximates concept	Cannot design mental model that illustrates rounding
Mathematical language (1)	Can list numerous situations in which exact number is not needed	Can list five situations in which exact number is not needed	Can list fewer than five situations in which exact number is not needed	Cannot name more than one situation in which exact number is not needed
Mathematical language (2)	Writes paragraph explaining rounding that could be used as example for classroom	Writes paragraph that adequately explains rounding	Writes paragraph explaining rounding with minimal assistance	Cannot explain rounding in writing with minimal assistance

www.ahaprocess.com

Absolute Value

A runner ran in a positive direction. He ran 6 feet.

$$|6| = 6$$

(The absolute value of 6 is 6.)

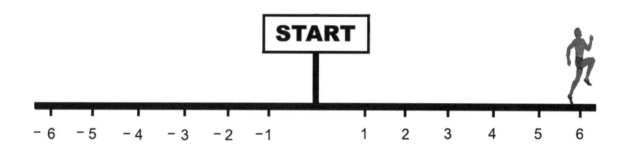

Another runner ran in a negative direction. He also ran 6 feet.

$$|-6| = 6$$

(The absolute value of negative 6 is 6.)

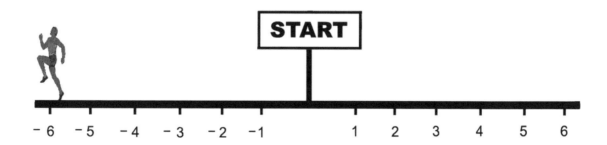

Absolute Value

A dirty car makes a <u>negative</u> impression.

When a dirty car goes into a car wash, <u>it changes</u>. It comes out clean.

A clean car makes a <u>positive</u> impression.

$$| \text{-}6 | = 6$$

A clean car makes a <u>positive</u> impression.

When a clean car goes into a car wash, <u>it does not change</u>. When it comes out it is still clean.

A clean car makes a <u>positive</u> impression.

$$| 6 | = 6$$

www.ahaprocess.com

MENTAL MODEL—NUMBERS AND OPERATIONS

Standard: Numbers and Operations

Understand numbers, ways of representing numbers, relationships among numbers, and number systems.

Compare and contrast the properties of numbers and number systems, including the rational and real numbers.

STEP SHEET

1. Read the mental model.
2. Write an explanation of the model in your own words or tell another student your explanation.
3. Choose a term (number and/or variable). Find its absolute value.
4. Create your own mental model for absolute value.
5. Explain your mental model to another student.

RUBRIC

Standard: Numbers and Operations

Understand numbers, ways of representing numbers, relationships among numbers, and number systems.

Compare and contrast the properties of numbers and number systems, including the rational and real numbers.

Criteria	4 Exceeds Standard	3 Meets Standard	2 Is Below Standard	1 Does Not Meet Standard
Relationships among numbers	Can identify absolute value of any term independently	Can identify absolute value of given terms independently	Can identify absolute value of given terms with minimal assistance	Cannot identify absolute value of given terms with minimal assistance
Mental model	Develops mental model that could be used as example for classroom	Develops adequate personal mental model	Develops mental model that encompasses portion of concept	Cannot develop mental model that explains concept
Process	Can explain absolute value to others	Can explain absolute-value process outlined in poster	Can identify absolute value when process is explained	Cannot identify absolute value when process is explained

www.ahaprocess.com

Ratio Ray

Ray has two eyes for every one nose, so the ratio of eyes to noses is 2 to 1. This ratio can be written 2 to 1, 2:1 or $\frac{2}{1}$.

Ears to eyes = 2:2; 2 to 2; $\frac{2}{2}$

Noses to mouths = 1:1; 1 to 1; $\frac{1}{1}$

Eyes to mouths = 2:1; 2 to 1; $\frac{2}{1}$

Noses to ears = 1:2; 1 to 2; $\frac{1}{2}$

Proportion

Ratio Ray and Plutonia from Pluto are proportional!

Ray's eyes to mouths (2:1) are proportional to Plutonia's eyes to mouths (4:2).

$$2:1 = 4:2$$

$$\text{Also,} \quad \frac{2}{1} = \frac{4}{2}$$

Ray's noses to ears (1:2) are proportional to Plutonia's noses to ears (2:4).

$$1:2 = 2:4$$

$$\text{Also,} \quad \frac{2}{1} = \frac{2}{4}$$

Proportional relationships have equal cross products.

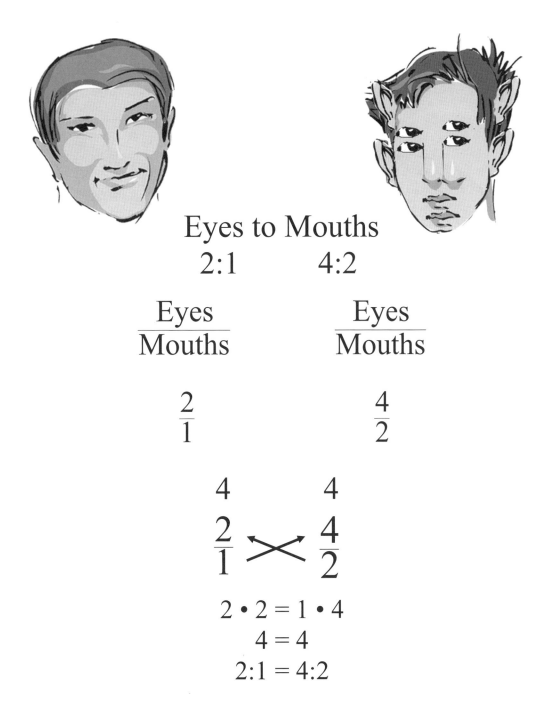

Eyes to Mouths
2:1   4:2

$$\frac{\text{Eyes}}{\text{Mouths}} \qquad \frac{\text{Eyes}}{\text{Mouths}}$$

$$\frac{2}{1} \qquad\qquad \frac{4}{2}$$

$$\overset{4}{\underset{}{\frac{2}{1}}} \times \overset{4}{\underset{}{\frac{4}{2}}}$$

$$2 \cdot 2 = 1 \cdot 4$$
$$4 = 4$$
$$2:1 = 4:2$$

A proportion is an equation with a ratio on each side. It is a statement that two ratios are equal.

Proportion

Ray and NaPortia from Neptune are ***not*** proportional.

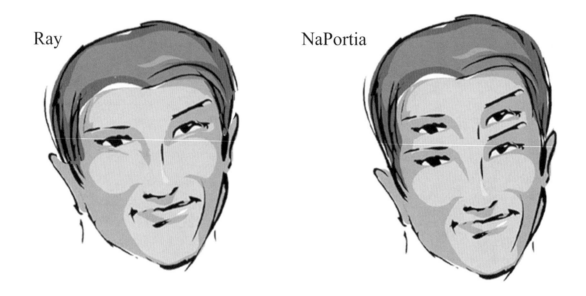

The ratio of Ray's eyes to mouths (2:1) is ***not*** proportional to NaPortia's eyes to mouths (4:1).

$$2{:}1 \neq 4{:}1$$
$$\frac{2}{1} \neq \frac{4}{1}$$

The ratio of Ray's eyes to ears (2:2) is ***not*** proportional to NaPortia's eyes to ears (4:2).

$$2{:}2 \neq 4{:}2$$
$$\frac{2}{2} \neq \frac{4}{2}$$

Non-proportional relationships *do not* have equal cross products.

Eyes to Mouths

2:1   4:1

$$\frac{\text{Eyes}}{\text{Mouths}} \qquad \frac{\text{Eyes}}{\text{Mouths}}$$

$$\frac{2}{1} \qquad\qquad \frac{4}{1}$$

$$\frac{2}{1} \diagdown\!\!\!\diagup \frac{4}{1}$$

$$1 \cdot 2 \neq 1 \cdot 4$$
$$2 \neq 4$$
$$2{:}1 \neq 4{:}1$$

Ray's and June's eyes and ears are proportional.

June from Jupiter has four ears. How many eyes does she have?

Eyes to Ears

2:2   n:4

$$\frac{\text{Eyes}}{\text{Ears}} \qquad \frac{\text{Eyes}}{\text{Ears}}$$

$$\frac{2}{2} \diagdown\diagup \frac{n}{4}$$

$$4 \cdot 2 = 2 \cdot n$$

$$8 = 2n$$

$$\frac{8}{2} = \frac{2n}{2}$$

$$4 = n$$

June has four eyes.

MENTAL MODEL—NUMBERS AND OPERATIONS

Standard: Numbers and Operations

Understand numbers, ways of representing numbers, relationships among numbers, and number systems.

Understand and use ratios and proportions to represent quantitative relationships.

Explanation of Mental Model:

This "poster style" mental model is designed for frequent viewing.

STEP SHEET

1. The ratio of your mouth to eyes is 1:2. List three additional ratios of your facial features (mouths, eyes, ears, eyebrows, noses).
2. Study the mental model and write the definition of *proportional* in your own words.
3. Study Mental Model #1 and explain in your own words how you know that Ray's and Plutonia's faces are proportional.
4. Study Mental Model #2 and explain in your own words how you know that Ray's and NaPortia's faces are not proportional.
5. Study Mental Model #3 and compute the number of eyes that June from Jupiter has.
6. Draw a space creature's face that has features that are proportional to yours.
7. Draw a face that has proportional features but has a different number of eyes than you have.
8. Create other space creatures and let your neighbor determine which ones have features that are numerically proportional to yours.
9. Design a mental model that explains ratio and proportion.

RUBRIC

Standard: Numbers and Operations

Understand numbers, ways of representing numbers, relationships among numbers, and number systems.

Understand and use ratios and proportions to represent quantitative relationships.

	4	3	2	1
Criteria	**Exceeds Standard**	**Meets Standard**	**Is Below Standard**	**Does Not Meet Standard**
Process	Designs sketches for others to compute (steps 6–8)	Computes ratios on sketches by others	Computes ratios on sketches by others with few mistakes	Cannot compute ratios on sketches
Computation	Can explain computations to others	Can compute number of eyes (step 5) independently	Can compute number of eyes (step 5) with minimal assistance	Cannot accurately compute number of eyes (step 5) with minimal assistance
Mathematical language	Writes definitions that could be used as examples for classroom	Writes appropriate definitions	Approximates accurate definitions	Cannot approximate definitions
Mental model	Designs mental model that could be used as example for classroom	Designs appropriate personal mental model	Designs mental model that approximates the concept	Cannot design appropriate mental model

Zero in Fractions

Please divide this pizza among the 8 people at the table.

But there is no pizza on the pan.

Well, their portions will be 0. Zero divided among any number is 0.

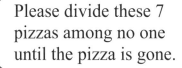

Please divide these 7 pizzas among no one until the pizza is gone.

But I would never finish. This would go on indefinitely.

You're right. It is <u>not</u> possible to divide something by nothing because it would go on for infinity.

We cannot have a 0 in the denominator of a fraction.

MENTAL MODEL—NUMBERS AND OPERATIONS

Standard: Numbers and Operations

Understand numbers, ways of representing numbers, relationships among numbers, and number systems.

Work flexibly with fractions, decimals, and percentages to solve problems.

Explanation of Mental Model:

This "poster style" mental model is designed for frequent viewing.

STEP SHEET

1. Review division problems and how they are checked:

   Problem: Eight divided by 4 equals 2.
   Proof: Two times 4 equals 8.

2. If a division problem had a zero in the denominator the answer could not be checked:

   Problem: Eight divided by 0 equals X.
   Proof: Zero times any number equals 0, so
               zero times X would equal 0, not 8.

   Conclusion: Division by 0 isn't possible.

3. Design a poster that illustrates why division by 0 isn't possible.

RUBRIC

Standard: Numbers and Operations

Understand numbers, ways of representing numbers, relationships among numbers, and number systems.

Work flexibly with fractions, decimals, and percentages to solve problems.

Criteria	4 **Exceeds Standard**	3 **Meets Standard**	2 **Is Below Standard**	1 **Does Not Meet Standard**
Process	Describes possible use of process in environment	Identifies process in example	Identifies process with minimal assistance	Cannot apply process with minimal assistance
Computation	Can assist others in computations	Performs computations accurately	Performs computations with minimal assistance	Cannot perform computations with minimal assistance
Mathematical language	Can explain to others why division by zero is not possible	Can give adequate explanation	Can give explanation with minimal assistance	Cannot explain why division by zero is not possible with minimal assistance
Mental model	Designs mental model that could be used as example for classroom	Designs appropriate personal mental model	Designs mental model that approximates the concept	Cannot design appropriate mental model

MENTAL MODEL—NUMBERS AND OPERATIONS

Standard: Numbers and Operations

Understand numbers, ways of representing numbers, relationships among numbers, and number systems.

Develop an understanding of large numbers and recognize and appropriately use exponential, scientific, and calculator notation.

Explanation of Mental Model:

This "poster style" mental model is designed for frequent viewing.

STEP SHEET

1. Compare figures on the two notes in the mental model.

2. Study the following notes, then define scientific notation in your own words:

   Scientists use **scientific notation** to express very large numbers. Scientific notation is based on powers of the base number 10. For example, the speed of light is 300,000,000 m/sec.

   The number 123,000,000,000 is written in scientific notation as: 1.23×10^{11}. *1.23* is called the coefficient of the number. The second number, called the base, must always be 10 in scientific notation.

   To write a number in scientific notation, put the decimal after the first digit and drop the zeroes. In the number 123,000,000,000 the coefficient will be 1.23.

   To find the exponent, count the number of places from the decimal to the last digit. In the number 123,000,000,000 there are 11 places.

   For small numbers we use a similar approach, but numbers smaller than 1 will have a negative exponent. A millionth of a second is:

   $$0.000001 \text{ sec. or } 1.0 \times 10^{-6}$$

3. Design a mental model that explains scientific notation.

RUBRIC

Standard: Numbers and Operations

Understand numbers, ways of representing numbers, relationships among numbers, and number systems.

Develop an understanding of large numbers and recognize and appropriately use exponential, scientific, and calculator notation.

	4	3	2	1
Criteria	**Exceeds Standard**	**Meets Standard**	**Is Below Standard**	**Does Not Meet Standard**
Process	Describes possible use of process in environment	Identifies purpose of process in example	Identifies purpose of process with minimal assistance	Cannot relay purpose of process with minimal assistance
Computation	Can assist others in computations	Performs computations accurately	Performs computations with minimal assistance	Cannot perform computations with minimal assistance
Mental model	Develops mental model that could be used as example for classroom	Develops appropriate personal mental model	Approximates appropriate mental model	Cannot develop appropriate mental model
Mathematical language	Writes definition that others understand	Writes appropriate personal definition of terms	Writes definition of terms with minimal assistance	Cannot define terms with minimal assistance

www.ahaprocess.com

Matrices

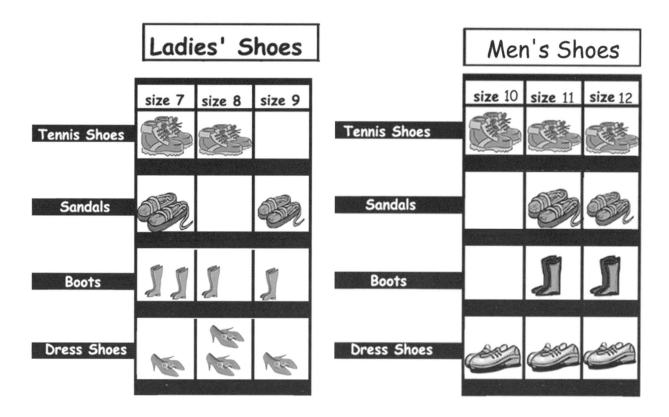

Following is a chart of what the Men's Shoes Matrix shows:

Type of Shoes	Size 10	Size 11	Size 12
Tennis	1 pair	1 pair	1 pair
Sandal	0	1 pair	1 pair
Boot	0	1 pair	1 pair
Dress	1 pair	1 pair	1 pair

Matrix notation for the above information:

$$\begin{bmatrix} 1 & 1 & 1 \\ 0 & 1 & 1 \\ 0 & 1 & 1 \\ 1 & 1 & 1 \end{bmatrix}$$

MENTAL MODEL—NUMBERS AND OPERATIONS

Standard: Numbers and Operations

Understand numbers, ways of representing numbers, relationships among numbers, and number systems.

Understand matrices as systems that have some of the properties of the real-number system.

Explanation of Mental Model:

This "poster style" mental model is designed to be used as a focal point for discussion of matrices.

STEP SHEET

1. Study the Matrices poster.

2. Following is a chart of what the Men's Shoes Matrix shows:

Type of Shoes	Size 10	Size 11	Size 12
Tennis	1 pair	1 pair	1 pair
Sandal	0	1 pair	1 pair
Boot	0	1 pair	1 pair
Dress	1 pair	1 pair	1 pair

   Make a chart of what the Ladies' Shoes Matrix shows.

3. Determine how many rows are in each matrix.

4. Determine how many columns are in each matrix.

   (The size of the matrix is defined by the number of **rows** and **columns**.) Answer: The above matrix has 4 rows and 3 columns. A matrix with m rows and n columns is an **(m x n)** (m by n) matrix. The first entry (m) is the number of rows; the second entry (n) represents the number of columns. The above matrix is a (4 x 3) matrix.

5. Determine how matrices would be added. (For example, one approach to adding matrices is to add entries **one by one.**)

6. Design a mental model explaining matrices.

RUBRIC

Standard: Numbers and Operations

Understand numbers, ways of representing numbers, relationships among numbers, and number systems.

Understand matrices as systems that have some of the properties of the real-number system.

Criteria	4 Exceeds Standard	3 Meets Standard	2 Is Below Standard	1 Does Not Meet Standard
Process	Describes possible use of process in environment	Identifies purpose of process in example	Identifies purpose of process with minimal assistance	Cannot relay purpose of process with minimal assistance
Computation	Can assist others in computations	Performs computations accurately	Performs computations with minimal assistance	Cannot perform computations with minimal assistance
Problem solving	Develops mental model that others understand	Develops appropriate personal mental model	Approximates appropriate mental model	Cannot develop appropriate mental model
Mathematical language	Defines terms in format that others understand	Writes appropriate personal definition of terms	Writes definition of terms with minimal assistance	Cannot define terms with minimal assistance

MENTAL MODEL—NUMBER SENSE, PROPERTIES, AND OPERATIONS

Standard: Multiplying Binomials

Algebra tiles paint a picture

Find the product of (2x + 3)(x + 4)

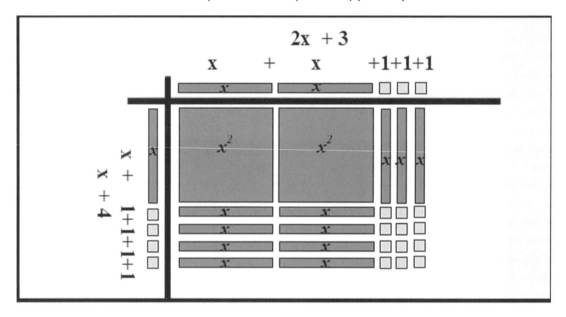

Explanation:

Algebra tiles are recommended as a concrete model for understanding algebraic operations. After students are comfortable using the tiles for addition and subtraction of positive and negative numbers, combining like terms, and multiplication of monomials, this model provides a smooth transition for multiplying binomials. As with all manipulative models, the three essential steps for students in the process are:

- Hands-on manipulation of the tiles
- Drawing a two-dimensional model of the process
- Connecting the process to the algorithm

Understanding of the algorithm of multiplication of two binomial expressions is important for algebraic fluency. Roots of this algorithm can be found in the process of multiplication of two-digit numbers.

MENTAL MODEL—NUMBERS AND OPERATIONS

Standard: Numbers and Operations

Compute with numbers (that is, add, subtract, multiply, divide).

Describe features of algorithms (such as regrouping with or without manipulatives, partial products).

STEP SHEET

1. Write the binomials to be multiplied.
2. Form a frame with length of the first binomial and width of the second binomial.
3. Select tiles to fill in the rectangle that have appropriate length and width.
4. Draw and label a picture of the results of the tile manipulation.
5. Identify the partial products from the tiles and in the drawing.
6. Combine like terms from the model.
7. Connect the model to the **Window** algorithm or the **FOIL** algorithm.

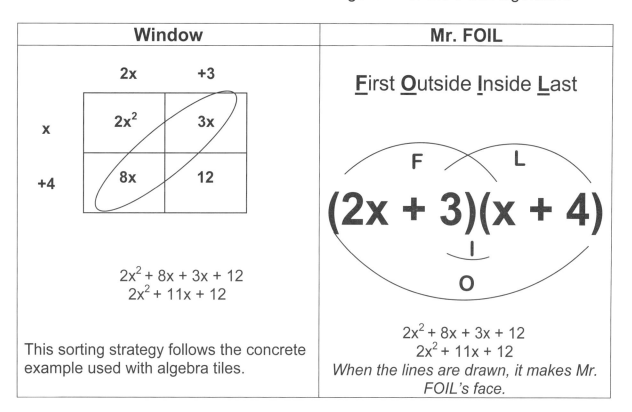

Window	**Mr. FOIL**
$2x$ $\quad$ $+3$ $2x^2$ $\quad$ $3x$ $8x$ $\quad$ 12 $2x^2 + 8x + 3x + 12$ $2x^2 + 11x + 12$ This sorting strategy follows the concrete example used with algebra tiles.	**F**irst **O**utside **I**nside **L**ast $(2x + 3)(x + 4)$ $2x^2 + 8x + 3x + 12$ $2x^2 + 11x + 12$ *When the lines are drawn, it makes Mr. FOIL's face.*

RUBRIC

Standard: Numbers and Operations

Compute with numbers (that is, add, subtract, multiply, divide).

Describe features of algorithms (such as regrouping with or without manipulatives, partial products).

Criteria	4 **Exceeds Standard**	3 **Meets Standard**	2 **Is Below Standard**	1 **Does Not Meet Standard**
Process	Uses more than one process to multiply binomials	Follows each step of given process	Follows each step of process with minimal assistance	Does not follow given process
Computation	Justifies correct solution	Makes no errors	Makes few errors in coefficients or exponents	Makes significant error(s)
Problem solving	Validates method and solution	Determines reasonableness of solution	Uses appropriate process correctly	Uses incorrect process
Mathematical language	Formal-language explanation of process	Consultative-language explanation of process	Labels parts of process	No explanation

 www.ahaprocess.com

LEAST COMMON DENOMINATOR
LEAST COMMON MULTIPLE

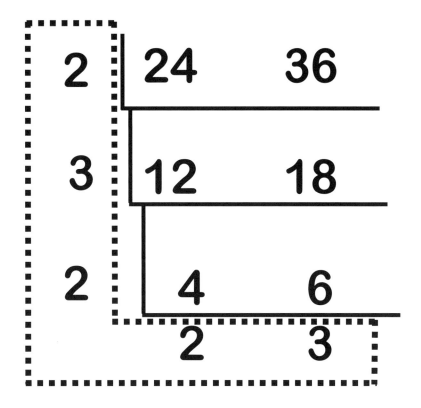

LCD or LCM = 2 • 3 • 2 • 2 • 3
LCD or LCM = 72

If 24 and 36 represented a fraction, $\frac{24}{36}$, then the last row is the fraction in lowest terms, $\frac{2}{3}$.

GREATEST COMMON FACTOR

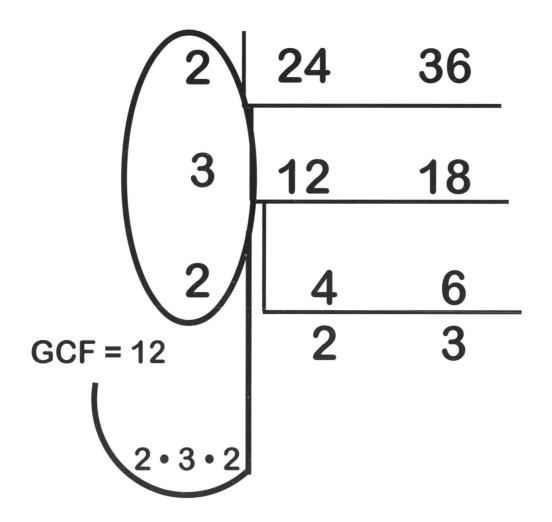

2	24	36
3	12	18
2	4	6
	2	3

GCF = 12

2 • 3 • 2

MENTAL MODEL—NUMBERS AND OPERATIONS

Standard: Numbers and Operations

Understand numbers, ways of representing numbers, relationships among numbers, and number systems.

The student represents and uses numbers in a variety of equivalent forms.

PROCESS for LCD or GCF

1. Look at the poster.

LCD

2. Write the two numbers to be factored.
3. Draw an upside-down division symbol (ladder).
4. Divide both numbers by a common factor. Write the factor to the left of the ladder.
5. Write the quotient beneath each dividend.
6. Repeat with steps until the only divisor common to both is 1. "When you get to 1, you are done!"
7. Since you are finding LCD (it starts with an "L"), draw a large block letter "L" around the factors/divisors on the left and the quotients on the bottom.
8. Multiply the numbers in the "L" to find the LCD/LCM.

GCF

2.–6. The same steps as above.
7. Since you are finding GCF (it starts with a "G"), draw the top of a lower-case "g" around the factors or divisors.
8. Draw the tail of the "g."
9. Multiply the factors/divisors together for the GCF.

STEP SHEET

1. Examine the poster.
2. List in your own words the steps for finding LCD or GCF.
3. Choose two terms of your own and make a poster illustrating the process for finding LCD or GCF.
4. Explain your poster to another student.

RUBRIC

Standard: Numbers and Operations

Understand numbers, ways of representing numbers, relationships among numbers, and number systems.

The student represents and uses numbers in a variety of equivalent forms.

Criteria	4 Exceeds Standard	3 Meets Standard	2 Is Below Standard	1 Does Not Meet Standard
Relationships among numbers	Applies process of finding LCD or GCF for any two terms independently	Can identify LCD or GCF of terms independently	Can identify LCD or GCF of given terms independently with minimal assistance	Cannot identify LCD or GCF of given terms with minimal assistance
Mathematical language	Accurately refers to LCD and GCF independently	Accurately refers to LCD or GCF while using poster	Refers to LCD or GCF with few errors	Cannot describe or refer to LCD or GCF
Computation	Can explain calculation of LCD or GCF of two terms to others	Can accurately calculate LCD or GCF of two terms independently	Can accurately calculate LCD or GCF of two terms with minimal assistance	Cannot accurately calculate LCD or GCF of two terms with minimal assistance
Process	Uses personal step sheet to show how to find LCD or GCF to others	Can explain process for finding LCD or GCF outlined in poster	Can identify LCD or GCF when process is explained	Cannot identify LCD or GCF when process is explained

     www.ahaprocess.com

Story Mental Model

MULTIPLICATION AND DIVISION OF INTEGERS

+ Good guy − Bad guy	+ Coming to town − Leaving town	Get
+ + − −	+ − + −	+ − − +

MENTAL MODEL—NUMBERS AND OPERATIONS

Standard: Numbers and Operations

Compute with numbers (add, subtract, multiply, divide).

Describe features of algorithms (such as regrouping with or without manipulatives, partial products).

Explanation of Mental Model:

Understanding how to multiply two-digit numbers is important for algebraic fluency.

STEP SHEET

1. Study the chart. Notice, the + sign in the first column represents good guys and the − sign represents bad guys. The + sign in the second column represents coming to town and the − sign represents leaving town.
2. Tell the story that the signs represent:
   When good guys (+) come to town (+), this is good (+).
   When bad guys (-) come to town (+), this is bad (-).
   When good guys (+) leave town (-), this is bad (-).
   When bad guys (-) leave town(-), this is good (+).
3. Write a paragraph explaining how to multiply signed numbers.
4. Substitute numerals in place of the good guys, bad, guys, etc., and compute the product. (If four good guys come to town eight times the result is _____.)
5. Write another story that helps you to remember how to multiply signed numbers.

Note for teachers: Story mental models provide a powerful memory tool for students. It is important, however, for students to understand the relationship between the story and the algorithm.

RUBRIC

Standard: Numbers and Operations

Compute with numbers (add, subtract, multiply, divide).

Describe features of algorithms (such as regrouping with or without manipulatives, partial products).

Criteria	**4** **Exceeds Standard**	**3** **Meets Standard**	**2** **Is Below Standard**	**1** **Does Not Meet Standard**
Process	Writes story mental model that could be used as example for classroom	Writes accurate story mental model for multiplying signed numbers	Writes story mental model with minimal assistance	Cannot write story mental model with minimal assistance
Computation	Can explain multiplication of signed numbers to others	Multiplies signed numbers with no errors	Multiplies signed numbers with few errors	Cannot multiply signed numbers accurately
Problem solving	Can explain problem-solving process to others	Follows problem-solving process with no errors	Follows problem-solving process with few errors	Cannot follow problem-solving process
Mathematical language	Writes paragraph that could be used as example for classroom	Writes accurate paragraph explaining how to multiply signed numbers	Writes paragraph explaining multiplication of signed numbers with minimal assistance	Cannot write paragraph explaining how to multiply signed numbers with minimal assistance

Multiplying and Dividing Integers

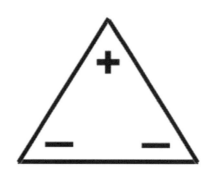

EXAMPLE	MENTAL MODEL DRAWING
(-2) (3)	
$\dfrac{-2}{-3}$	
(x) (-y)	

MENTAL MODEL—NUMBERS AND OPERATIONS

Standard: Numbers and Operations

Compute with numbers (add, subtract, multiply, divide).

Describe features of algorithms (such as regrouping with or without manipulatives, partial products).

Explanation of Mental Model:

Understanding how to multiply two-digit numbers is important for algebraic fluency.

STEP SHEET

1. Draw a triangle on a sheet of paper.
2. In two corners write a negative sign (-).
3. In one corner write a positive sign (+).
4. When multiplying or dividing two integers, cover the corners that match the signs of the two integers to determine the sign of the answer.
5. Write a paragraph explaining why this mental model is true.

RUBRIC

Standard: Numbers and Operations

Compute with numbers (that is, add, subtract, multiply, divide).

Describe features of algorithms (such as regrouping with or without manipulatives, partial products).

	4	3	2	1
Criteria	**Exceeds Standard**	**Meets Standard**	**Is Below Standard**	**Does Not Meet Standard**
Process	Develops a new process for multiplying and dividing integers	Uses given process accurately	Follows each step of given process with some assistance	Cannot follow each step of given process with minimal assistance
Computation	Can explain computations to others	Computes with no errors	Computes with few significant errors	Computes with significant errors
Problem solving	Explains problem-solving process to others	Follows problem-solving process with no errors	Follows problem-solving process with few errors	Cannot follow problem-solving process with minimal assistance
Mathematical language	Writes paragraph explaining validity of this mental model that could be used as example for classroom	Writes accurate paragraph explaining why this mental model is true	Writes paragraph explaining this mental model with minimal assistance	Cannot write paragraph explaining validity of this mental model with minimal assistance

www.ahaprocess.com

MENTAL MODEL

Addition and Subtraction of Integers

● = positive integer
"in the black"   ○ = negative integer   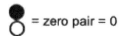 = zero pair = 0

Combining	Addition and Subtraction
2 - 3 **2 + (-3)**	**2 - 3**
1. Build 2.	1. Build 2.
2. Combine with -3.	2. Can I take 3 away? NO
3. Cancel zero pairs.	3. Why? What do I need to make 3? 1 MORE
4. Record the solution. 2 - 3 = -1	4. How can that be done?
	5. Add one zero pair.
	6. Take away 3.
	7. Record the solution. 2 - 3 = -1

Addition and Subtraction of Integers

● = positive integer "in the black"   ○ = negative integer   ⦵ = zero pair = 0

Combining	Addition and Subtraction
(-2) - 3	(-2) - 3
(-3) + 2	(-3) + 2
(-2) - (-3)	(-2) - (-3)

   www.ahaprocess.com

MENTAL MODEL—NUMBERS AND OPERATIONS

Standard: Numbers and Operations

Compute with numbers (add, subtract, multiply, divide).

Describe features of algorithms (such as regrouping with or without manipulatives, partial products).

STEP SHEET

1. Read each step of the combining strategy on page one of the mental model.
2. Reproduce each step on a sheet of paper.
3. Read each step of the addition and subtraction strategy on page one of the mental model.
4. Reproduce each step on a sheet of paper.
5. Follow each step of both strategies to solve the addition problems on page two of the mental model.
6. Decide which strategy you like best.
7. Write a paragraph explaining why you selected the one you did.

RUBRIC

Standard: Numbers and Operations

Compute with numbers (add, subtract, multiply, divide).

Describe features of algorithms (such as regrouping with or without manipulatives, partial products).

Criteria	4 Exceeds Standard	3 Meets Standard	2 Is Below Standard	1 Does Not Meet Standard
Process	Can explain steps of process to others	Follows each step of process	Follows each step of process with minimal assistance	Cannot follow steps of process with minimal assistance
Computation	Can explain computations to others	Computes with no errors	Computes with few significant errors	Computes with significant error(s)
Problem solving	Applies computations to problem solving outside classwork	Applies computations to problem solving in classwork	Applies computations to problem solving in classwork with minimal assistance	Cannot apply computations with minimal assistance
Mathematical language	Writes paragraph that could be used as example for classroom	Writes accurate paragraph validating choice	Writes paragraph with minimal assistance	Cannot write paragraph validating choice with minimal assistance

CHAPTER TWO
Algebra

$$y = x$$

I want to be just like you.   I am an independent adult.
                                    You can depend on me!

Dependent Variable   **Independent Variable**

NOTE: Some mathematicians avoid use of this terminology because of possible confusion with other disciplines.

www.ahaprocess.com

MENTAL MODEL—ALGEBRA

Standard: Algebra

Represent and analyze mathematical situations and structures using algebraic symbols.

Develop an initial conceptual understanding of different uses of variables.

Explanation of Mental Model:

This "poster style" mental model is designed for frequent viewing.

STEP SHEET

1. Study the mental model about dependent and independent variables.
2. Write in your own words a definition of dependent and independent variables.
3. Find equations in your textbook that contain dependent and independent variables.
4. Create a poster that explains dependent and independent variables.

RUBRIC

Standard: Algebra

Represent and analyze mathematical situations and structures using algebraic symbols.

Develop an initial conceptual understanding of different uses of variables.

Criteria	4 Exceeds Standard	3 Meets Standard	2 Is Below Standard	1 Does Not Meet Standard
Process	Identifies examples of dependent and independent variables in environment	Identifies examples of dependent and independent variables in textbook	Identifies examples of dependent and independent variables in textbook with minimal assistance	Cannot identify dependent and independent variables in textbook with minimal assistance
Mental model	Designs mental model that could be used as example for classroom	Designs accurate personal mental model	Designs mental model with minimal assistance	Cannot design accurate mental model with minimal assistance
Mathematical language	Can explain dependent and independent variables to others	Writes accurate definitions of dependent and independent variables	Writes accurate definitions of dependent and independent variables with minimal assistance	Cannot write definitions with minimal assistance

www.ahaprocess.com

Inequalities

Example: $2x + 5 \leq 7$

$(2x + 5) - 5 \leq 7 - 5$

$2x \leq 2$

$$\frac{2x}{2} \leq \frac{2}{2}$$

$x \leq 1$

MENTAL MODEL—ALGEBRA

Standard: Algebra

Represent and analyze mathematical situations and structures using algebraic symbols to express mathematical relationships using equations.

Represent and analyze mathematical situations and structures using algebraic symbols.

Understand the meaning of equivalent forms of expressions, equations, inequalities, and relations.

Explanation of Mental Model:

This "poster style" mental model is designed for frequent viewing.

STEP SHEET

1. Study the mental model.
2. Write your own definition of inequality.
3. Write word problems that contain inequalities.
4. Write four multiple-choice answers to your word problems.
   Only one response can be correct.
   One response must be funny.
5. Give your question to one of your friends to answer.
6. Create your own mental model to illustrate inequalities.

RUBRIC

Standard: Algebra

Represent and analyze mathematical situations and structures using algebraic symbols to express mathematical relationships using equations.

Represent and analyze mathematical situations and structures using algebraic symbols.

Understand the meaning of equivalent forms of expressions, equations, inequalities, and relations.

	4	3	2	1
Criteria	**Exceeds Standard**	**Meets Standard**	**Is Below Standard**	**Does Not Meet Standard**
Mental model	Develops mental model that could be used as example for classroom	Develops appropriate personal mental model	Develops mental model with minimal assistance	Cannot develop mental model with minimal assistance
Computation	Correctly critiques peers' questions	Correctly answers peers' questions	Answers peers' questions with minimal assistance	Cannot answer peers' questions with minimal assistance
Problem solving	Writes word problems for others to solve	Writes reasonable word problem	Writes word problem with minimal assistance	Cannot write word problem with minimal assistance

Proportionality—The Box

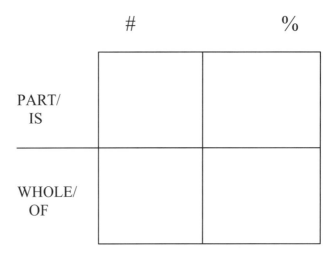

	#	%
PART/ IS		
WHOLE/ OF		

The Box

This model is used for every type of proportionality problem.

Example: Bob runs the 50-meter dash in 45 seconds. How many meters does he run in one second?

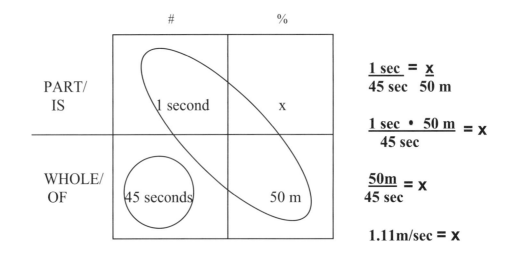

$$\frac{1 \text{ sec}}{45 \text{ sec}} = \frac{x}{50 \text{ m}}$$

$$\frac{1 \text{ sec} \cdot 50 \text{ m}}{45 \text{ sec}} = x$$

$$\frac{50 \text{m}}{45 \text{ sec}} = x$$

$$1.11 \text{m/sec} = x$$

Adapted from Alvin Independent School District math training materials

MENTAL MODEL—ALGEBRA

Standard: Algebra

Represent and analyze mathematical situations and structures using algebraic symbols to express mathematical relationships using equations.

STEP SHEET

1. Draw and label the box.
2. Fill the numbers and unknowns in the boxes.
3. Cross-multiply. Circle the "bat."
4. Divide by the "ball."
5. Substitute other numbers in the example.
6. Work the new problem.
7. Write additional problems for your friends to solve.

RUBRIC

Standard: Algebra

Represent and analyze mathematical situations and structures using algebraic symbols to express mathematical relationships using equations.

Criteria	4 Exceeds Standard	3 Meets Standard	2 Is Below Standard	1 Does Not Meet Standard
Process	Can explain process to others	Follows process independently	Follows process with minimal assistance	Cannot follow process with minimal assistance
Computation	Can explain computations to peers	Correctly computes peers' problems	Computes peers' problems with minimal assistance	Cannot compute peers' problems with minimal assistance
Problem solving	Writes word problems for others to solve	Writes reasonable word problem	Writes word problem with minimal assistance	Cannot write word problem with minimal assistance

www.ahaprocess.com

If every element in the domain is paired with exactly one element in the range (there is one arrow going in one direction), the relation is a function.

If elements in the domain are paired with more than one element in the range (there is more than one arrow going in one direction), the relation is not a function.

MENTAL MODEL—ALGEBRA

Standard: Algebra

Understand patterns, relations, and functions.

Identify functions as linear or nonlinear and contrast their properties from tables, graphs, or equations.

Explanation of Mental Model:

This "poster style" mental model is designed for frequent viewing.

STEP SHEET

1. Study the arrows in the words and phrases on the poster.
   Note: There is one arrow in the word, *function*, and two arrows in the phrase, *not a function.*
2. Read about functions in your text.
3. Write mathematical statements and ask your neighbor to identify those that are functions and those that are not.
4. Develop a mental model of your own to explain functions.
5. When studying functions in class, use this mental model or your own mental model as an aid in remembering the definition of a function.

www.ahaprocess.com

RUBRIC

Standard: Algebra

Understand patterns, relations, and functions.

Identify functions as linear or nonlinear and contrast their properties from tables, graphs, or equations.

	4	3	2	1
Criteria	**Exceeds Standard**	**Meets Standard**	**Is Below Standard**	**Does Not Meet Standard**
Mental model	Develops mental model that could be used as example for classroom	Develops accurate personal mental model	Develops mental model with minimal assistance	Cannot develop mental model with minimal assistance
Computation	Correctly critiques peers' written functions	Correctly identifies peers' written functions	Identifies peers' written functions with minimal assistance	Cannot write or identify written functions with minimal assistance
Problem solving	Writes word functions for others to identify	Can write sample word functions	Can write word functions with minimal assistance	Cannot write word functions with minimal assistance

Give your graphs the

Vertical
One-Touch Function
Test

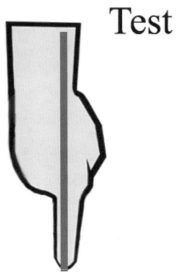

If a vertical line touches only one point on a graphed line or curve, it is a function.

If a vertical line touches more than one point on a graphed line or curve, it is not a function.

Examples:

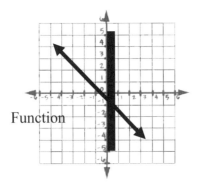

Function

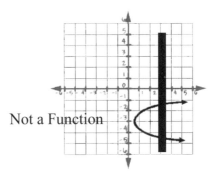

Not a Function

MENTAL MODEL—ALGEBRA

Standard: Algebra

Understand patterns, relations, and functions.

Identify functions as linear or nonlinear and contrast their properties from tables, graphs, or equations.

Explanation of Mental Model:

This "poster style" mental model is designed for frequent viewing.

STEP SHEET

1. Study the mental model.
2. Write a paragraph explaining in your own words the Vertical One-Touch Function Test.
3. Draw graphed lines and ask your neighbor to identify those that are functions and those that are not.

RUBRIC

Standard: Algebra

Understand patterns, relations, and functions.

Identify functions as linear or nonlinear and contrast their properties from tables, graphs, or equations.

Criteria	4 Exceeds Standard	3 Meets Standard	2 Is Below Standard	1 Does Not Meet Standard
Mathematical language	Writes paragraph explaining One-Touch Function Test that could be used as example for classroom	Writes paragraph accurately explaining One-Touch Function Test	Writes paragraph explaining One-Touch Function Test with minimal assistance	Cannot write paragraph explaining One-Touch Function Test with minimal assistance
Computation	Correctly critiques peers' graphs	Correctly identifies peers' graphed functions	Identifies peers' graphed functions with minimal assistance	Cannot write or identify graphed functions with minimal assistance
Problem solving	Draws graph lines that could be included on test	Draws accurate graph lines for others to identify	Draws graph lines with minimal assistance	Cannot draw accurate graph lines with minimal assistance

www.ahaprocess.com

Functions

A function can be "walked."

Non-functions cannot be "walked" without turning upside-down or walking straight up a "wall."

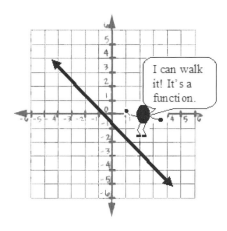

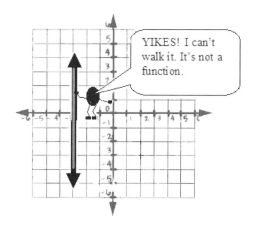

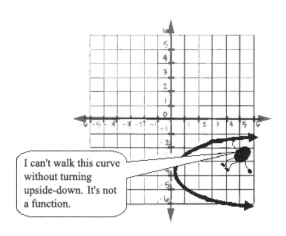

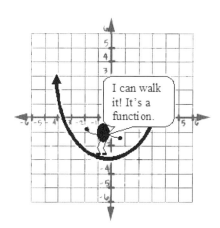

MENTAL MODEL—ALGEBRA

Standard: Algebra

Understand patterns, relations, and functions.

Identify functions as linear or nonlinear and contrast their properties from tables, graphs, or equations.

Explanation of Mental Model:

This "poster style" mental model is designed for frequent viewing.

STEP SHEET

1. Study the mental model.
2. Write a paragraph explaining how to identify functions using the "walk" procedure.
3. Draw graphed lines and ask your neighbor to identify those that are functions and those that are not.

RUBRIC

Standard: Algebra

Understand patterns, relations, and functions.

Identify functions as linear or nonlinear and contrast their properties from tables, graphs, or equations.

Criteria	4 Exceeds Standard	3 Meets Standard	2 Is Below Standard	1 Does Not Meet Standard
Mathematical language	Writes paragraph explaining "walk" procedure that could be used as example for classroom	Writes paragraph accurately explaining "walk" procedure	Writes paragraph explaining "walk" procedure with minimal assistance	Cannot write paragraph explaining "walk" procedure with minimal assistance
Computation	Correctly critiques peers' graphs	Correctly identifies peers' graphed functions	Identifies peers' graphed functions with minimal assistance	Cannot write or identify graphed functions with minimal assistance
Problem solving	Draws graph lines that could be included on test	Draws accurate graph lines for others to identify	Draws accurate graph lines with minimal assistance	Cannot draw accurate graph lines with minimal assistance

Interval Notation

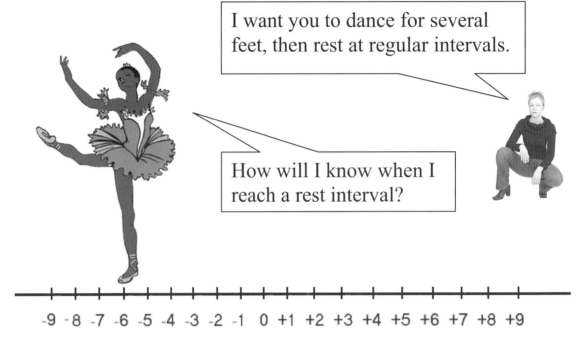

Interval Notation

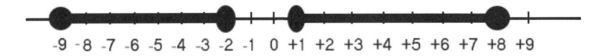

www.ahaprocess.com

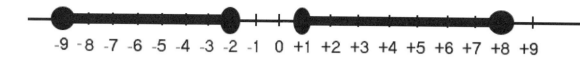

MENTAL MODEL—ALGEBRA

Standard: Algebra

Use number lines as representational tools.

STEP SHEET

1. Study the poster on Interval Notation.
2. Study the following example of Interval Notation and solve the problem. (The answer is below.)

Solve $|2x+3| < 4$

A.

B.

C.
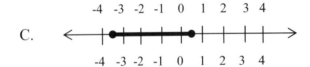

3. Define interval notation in your own words.
4. Develop a mental model that illustrates Interval Notation.
5. Define union in your own words.
6. Develop a mental model that illustrates union.
7. The answer to the example Interval Notation problem is A.

www.ahaprocess.com

RUBRIC

Standard: Algebra

Understand numbers, ways of representing numbers, relationships among numbers, and number systems.

Compare and order fractions, decimals, and percentages efficiently and find their approximate locations on a number line.

Criteria	4 Exceeds Standard	3 Meets Standard	2 Is Below Standard	1 Does Not Meet Standard
Process	Describes possible use of process in environment	Identifies purpose of process	Identifies purpose of process with minimal assistance	Cannot relay purpose of process with minimal assistance
Computation	Can interpret mental model for others	Interprets mental model accurately for self	Interprets poster accurately with minimal assistance	Cannot interpret mental model with minimal assistance
Problem solving	Develops mental model that could be used as example for classroom	Develops accurate personal mental model	Develops accurate mental model with minimal assistance	Cannot develop accurate mental model with minimal assistance
Mathematical language	Writes definitions that others understand	Writes accurate personal definitions of terms	Writes accurate definitions of terms with minimal assistance	Cannot define terms with minimal assistance

You must crawl before you can stand.

The horizontal distance of a point (x,y) is graphed first:

x = horizontal distance = crawl
y = vertical distance = stand

Example:

Graph the point (2,3) or

x	y
2	3

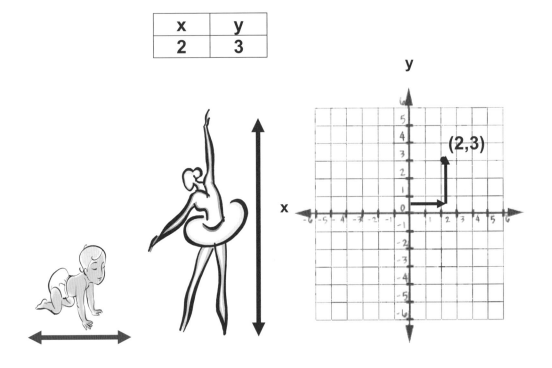

www.ahaprocess.com

MENTAL MODEL—ALGEBRA

Standard: Algebra

Use number lines and rectangular coordinate systems as representational tools.

Identify or graph sets of points on a number line or in a rectangular coordinate system.

STEP SHEET

1. On graph paper, draw x-axis and y-axis.
2. Practice moving positive and negative distance on the x-axis (horizontally) and on the y-axis (vertically).
3. Graph and label points (x,y) on a coordinate grid.

RUBRIC

Standard: Algebra

Use number lines and rectangular coordinate systems as representational tools.

Identify or graph sets of points on a number line or in a rectangular coordinate systems.

	4	3	2	1
Criteria	**Exceeds Standard**	**Meets Standard**	**Is Below Standard**	**Does Not Meet Standard**
Process	Develops new process to solve problems	Follows each step of given process	Follows process with minimal assistance	Cannot follow given process with minimal assistance
Mathematical language	Recognizes and explains related topics	Gives in-depth explanation of labels	Uses correct labels inconsistently	Does not use labels correctly
Mental model	Develops mental model that could be used as example for classroom	Develops appropriate personal mental model	Develops mental model with minimal assistance	Cannot develop mental model with minimal assistance

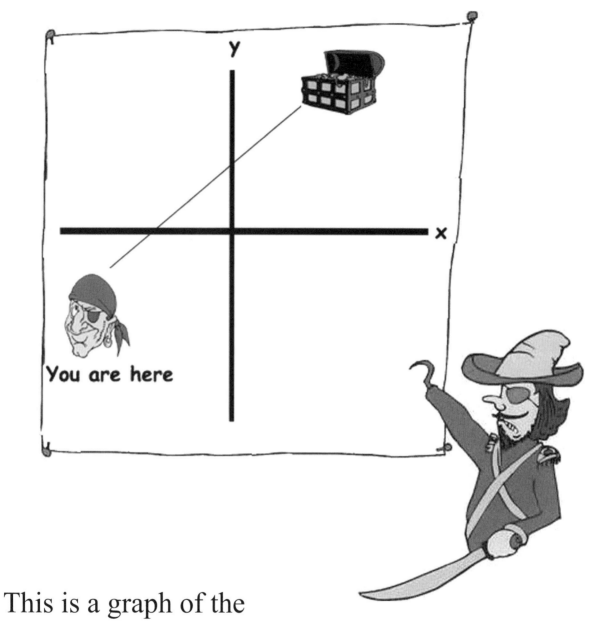

You are here

This is a graph of the

linear equation, y = mx + b

that we found on the treasure map.

A **line**ar equation means we will travel in
a straight **line**.

MENTAL MODEL—ALGEBRA

Standard: Algebra

Represent and analyze mathematical situations and structures using algebraic symbols.

Use symbolic algebra to represent situations and to solve problems, especially those that involve linear relationships.

Explanation of Mental Model:

This "poster style" mental model is designed for frequent viewing.

STEP SHEET

1. Study the mental model and write a definition of a linear equation in your own words.
2. Compare your definition with glossary definitions.
3. Create a poster that illustrates linear equations.

RUBRIC

Standard: Algebra

Represent and analyze mathematical situations and structures using algebraic symbols.

Use symbolic algebra to represent situations and to solve problems, especially those that involve linear relationships.

	4	3	2	1
Criteria	**Exceeds Standard**	**Meets Standard**	**Is Below Standard**	**Does Not Meet Standard**
Process	Can explain process of solving linear equations to others	Follows each step of given process	Follows process with some assistance	Does not follow given process
Mathematical language	Writes model definition of linear equation	Gives accurate definition of linear equation	Writes definition of linear equation with minimal assistance	Cannot write definition of linear equation with minimal assistance
Mental model	Develops mental model that could be used as example for classroom	Develops accurate personal mental model	Develops mental model with minimal assistance	Cannot develop mental model with minimal assistance

Linear Equation: y = m (slope) times x + b (y-intercept)

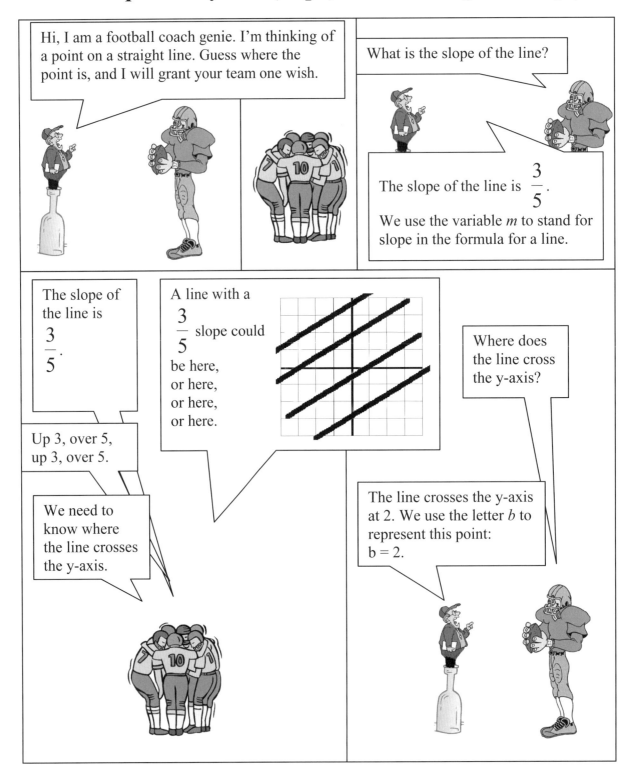

www.ahaprocess.com

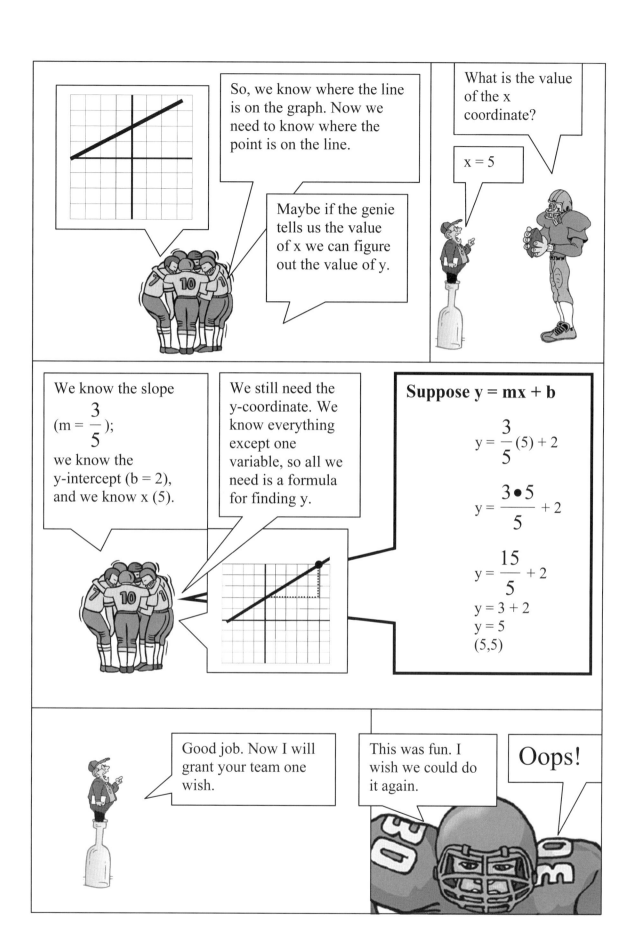

MENTAL MODEL—ALGEBRA

Standard: Algebra

Represent and analyze mathematical situations and structures using algebraic symbols.

Use symbolic algebra to represent situations and to solve problems, especially those that involve linear relationships.

Explanation of Mental Model:

This cartoon-style mental model logically explains the necessity of each component in the linear equation $y = mx + b$.

STEP SHEET

1. Read the cartoon.
2. Make a copy of the cartoon. On the copy, cover up the words in each bubble.
3. From recall, write the words that each character is saying.
4. Compare your words with the original cartoon.
5. Repeat until you can approximately reproduce each bubble.
6. Draw another cartoon using the same or a different theme involving another line or point on a line.

RUBRIC

Standard: Algebra

Represent and analyze mathematical situations and structures using algebraic symbols.

Use symbolic algebra to represent situations and to solve problems, especially those that involve linear relationships.

	4	3	2	1
Criteria	Exceeds Standard	Meets Standard	Is Below Standard	Does Not Meet Standard
Process	Develops new cartoon to describe linear equation	Reproduces character conversation in original cartoon	Reproduces character conversation in original cartoon with minimal assistance	Cannot reproduce conversation in original cartoon with minimal assistance
Computation	Illustrates correct solution in new cartoon	Makes no computational errors in new cartoon	Makes minor error(s) in new cartoon	Makes significant error(s) in new cartoon
Problem solving	Can explain linear equations to others	Can solve linear equations	Can understand explanation of linear equations	Cannot understand explanation of linear equations
Mathematical language	Recognizes and explains related topics	Gives in-depth explanation of labels	Uses labels correctly with few errors	Frequently uses labels incorrectly

QUADRUPLETS CAN FORM A *SQUARE* AND NOTHING MORE.

QUADRATIC EXPRESSIONS CONTAIN A *SQUARE* (x^2) AND NOTHING HIGHER.

Examples of quadratic expressions:

1. x^2
2. $z^2 + 3z$
3. $2x^2 + 3x - 5$
4. $a^2 - 1$
5. $p^2 - 4p - 6$

MENTAL MODEL—ALGEBRA

Standard: Algebra

Understand numbers, ways of representing numbers, relationships among numbers, and number systems.

Compare and contrast the properties of numbers and number systems, including the rational and real numbers, and understand complex numbers as solutions to quadratic equations that do not have real solutions.

Explanation of Mental Model:

This "poster style" mental model is designed for frequent viewing.

STEP SHEET

1. Look in a mathematics glossary and find a definition of the base *quad*.
2. Find words that contain the base *quad*. Read the definition of each word.
3. Study the word *quadratic*.
4. Study the mental model. Examine the examples of quadratic expressions and determine what they have in common.
5. Write additional quadratic expressions.
6. Design a mental model that explains quadratic expressions.

RUBRIC

Standard: Algebra

Understand numbers, ways of representing numbers, relationships among numbers, and number systems.

Compare and contrast the properties of numbers and number systems, including the rational and real numbers, and understand complex numbers as solutions to quadratic equations that do not have real solutions.

Criteria	4 Exceeds Standard	3 Meets Standard	2 Is Below Standard	1 Does Not Meet Standard
Process	Can clearly describe characteristics of quadratic expressions to others	Can describe characteristics of quadratic expressions	Describes characteristics of quadratic expressions with minimal assistance	Cannot describe characteristics of quadratic expressions with minimal assistance
Computation	Can explain quadratic expressions to others	Recognizes quadratic expressions	Can identify quadratic expressions with minimal assistance	Cannot identify quadratic expressions with minimal assistance
Mathematical language	Recognizes additional terms that are derived from same word bases	Gives in-depth explanation of labels	Uses labels correctly with some assistance	Uses labels incorrectly

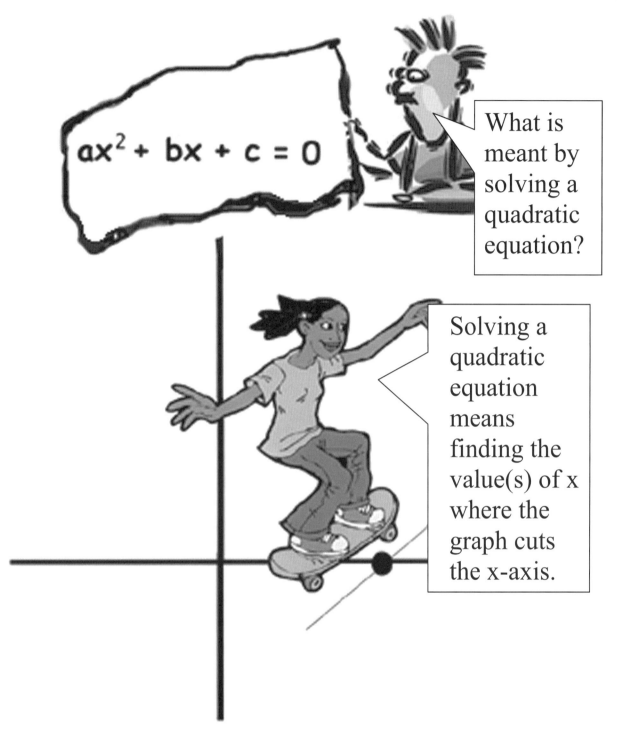

A **Quadratic Equation** is a second-degree polynomial equation in which the highest power of the unknown variable is 2. The most common **form** of a quadratic equation is where the right-hand side is set to zero.

MENTAL MODEL—ALGEBRA

Standard: Algebra

Understand numbers, ways of representing numbers, relationships among numbers, and number systems.

Compare and contrast the properties of numbers and number systems, including the rational and real numbers, and understand complex numbers as solutions to quadratic equations that do not have real solutions.

Explanation of Mental Model:

This "poster style" mental model is designed for frequent viewing.

STEP SHEET

1. Study the mental model. List the characteristics of a quadratic equation.
2. Compare your list with a glossary definition.
3. Write a multiple-choice question about quadratic equations, with the following specifications:
   a. Your stem must be in the form of a question.
   b. You must have four possible answers (a, b, c, and d).
   c. Only one answer can be correct.
   d. One distracter must be funny.
   e. You may not use "all of the above" or "none of the above."

RUBRIC

Standard: Algebra

Understand numbers, ways of representing numbers, relationships among numbers, and number systems.

Compare and contrast the properties of numbers and number systems, including the rational and real numbers, and understand complex numbers as solutions to quadratic equations that do not have real solutions.

	4	3	2	1
Criteria	**Exceeds Standard**	**Meets Standard**	**Is Below Standard**	**Does Not Meet Standard**
Mathematical language (1)	Lists more than one characteristic of quadratic equations	Lists one characteristic of quadratic equations	Lists one characteristic of quadratic equations with minimal assistance	Cannot list any characteristics of linear equations with minimal assistance
Mathematical language (2)	Develops multiple-choice question that could be included on test	Develops multiple-choice question, following guidelines	Develops multiple-choice question with minimal assistance	Cannot develop multiple-choice question with minimal assistance
Problem solving	Can explain quadratic equations	Can identify quadratic equations	Can understand explanation of quadratic equations	Cannot understand explanation of quadratic equations

Honey! What do I feed the baby?

The formula is on the refrigerator.

Honey! How do I balance the checkbook?

The formula is on the desk.

Honey! How do I solve a quadratic equation?

Use the quadratic formula:

$$x = \frac{-b \pm \sqrt{b^2 - 4ac}}{2a}$$

MENTAL MODEL—ALGEBRA

Standard: Algebra

Understand numbers, ways of representing numbers, relationships among numbers, and number systems.

Compare and contrast the properties of numbers and number systems, including the rational and real numbers, and understand complex numbers as solutions to quadratic equations that do not have real solutions.

Explanation of Mental Model:

This "poster style" mental model is designed for frequent viewing.

STEP SHEET

1. Study the mental model.
2. Reproduce the cartoon and "white out" the words in the conversation bubbles.
3. Rewrite the words in the bubbles from memory.
4. Create a cartoon or mental model showing that the purpose of the quadratic formula is to solve quadratic equations.
5. Develop a mental model that explains each step of the quadratic formula.

RUBRIC

Standard: Algebra

Understand numbers, ways of representing numbers, relationships among numbers, and number systems.

Compare and contrast the properties of numbers and number systems, including the rational and real numbers, and understand complex numbers as solutions to quadratic equations that do not have real solutions.

	4	3	2	1
Criteria	**Exceeds Standard**	**Meets Standard**	**Is Below Standard**	**Does Not Meet Standard**
Mathematical language	Can reproduce cartoon fully	Can approximately reproduce cartoon	Can reproduce cartoon with minimal assistance	Cannot reproduce cartoon with minimal assistance
Mental model	Develops mental model that explains quadratic formula	Develops mental model that explains purpose of quadratic formula	Can develop mental model that explains purpose of quadratic formula with minimal assistance	Cannot develop mental model that explains purpose of quadratic formula with minimal assistance
Problem solving	Can explain quadratic formula	Can identify quadratic formula	Can understand explanation of quadratic formula with minimal assistance	Cannot understand explanation of quadratic formula with minimal assistance

Introducing the new
Sloper-Size Machine

The *run* is 8 feet.

You set the *rise*!
(Sloper-Size me!!)

$\frac{1}{8}$ slope

Rise = 1, Run = 8

$\frac{2}{8}$ slope

Rise = 2, Run = 8

$\frac{3}{8}$ slope

Rise = 3, Run = 8

$\frac{4}{8}$ slope

Rise = 4, Run = 8

$\frac{5}{8}$ slope

Rise = 5, Run = 8

MENTAL MODEL—ALGEBRA

Standard: Algebra

Represent and analyze mathematical situations and structures using algebraic symbols.

Explore relationships between symbolic expressions and graphs of lines, paying particular attention to the meaning of intercept and slope.

Explanation of Mental Model:

This "poster style" mental model is designed for frequent viewing.

STEP SHEET

1. Study the mental model. Write your own definition of slope.
2. Find a definition of slope in a mathematics textbook glossary.
3. Compare your definition with the textbook definition.
4. Using graph paper, sketch lines at various slopes.
5. Ask a friend to identify the slope of each line.
6. Create a poster that explains slope.

www.ahaprocess.com

RUBRIC

Standard: Algebra

Represent and analyze mathematical situations and structures using algebraic symbols.

Explore relationships between symbolic expressions and graphs of lines, paying particular attention to the meaning of intercept and slope.

	4	3	2	1
Criteria	Exceeds Standard	Meets Standard	Is Below Standard	Does Not Meet Standard
Computation	Critiques peers' graphs	Can compute slope of lines on peers' graphs	Can compute slope of lines on peers' graphs with minimal assistance	Cannot compute slope of lines on peers' graphs with minimal assistance
Problem solving	Develops graph problems that could be included on test	Develops graph problems for peers to solve	Develops graph problems for peers to solve with minimal assistance	Cannot graph problems for peers to solve with minimal assistance
Mental model	Develops mental model that could be used as example for classroom	Develops appropriate personal mental model	Develops mental model with minimal assistance	Cannot develop mental model with minimal assistance

Slope Formula

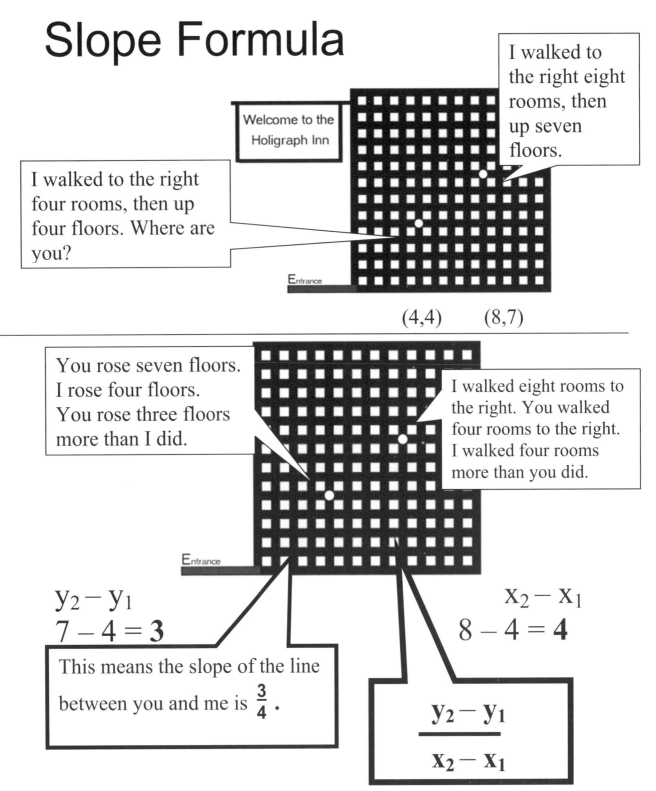

(4,4)　　(8,7)

$y_2 - y_1$
$7 - 4 = 3$

$x_2 - x_1$
$8 - 4 = 4$

$$\frac{y_2 - y_1}{x_2 - x_1}$$

　　www.ahaprocess.com

MENTAL MODEL—ALGEBRA

Standard: Algebra

Represent and analyze mathematical situations and structures using algebraic symbols.

Explore relationships between symbolic expressions and graphs of lines, paying particular attention to the meaning of intercept and slope.

Explanation of Mental Model:

This "poster style" mental model is designed for frequent viewing.

STEP SHEET

1. Study the mental model.
2. Make a copy of the cartoon. On the copy, cover up the words in the bubbles.
3. Reproduce the words in the bubbles from memory.
4. Compare the words in your bubbles with the originals.
5. Move the positions of the people in the hotel and change the words in the bubble to make them correct.
6. Develop another mental model that explains the formula for slope.

RUBRIC

Standard: Algebra

Represent and analyze mathematical situations and structures using algebraic symbols.

Explore relationships between symbolic expressions and graphs of lines, paying particular attention to the meaning of intercept and slope.

	4	3	2	1
Criteria	**Exceeds Standard**	**Meets Standard**	**Is Below Standard**	**Does Not Meet Standard**
Mathematical language	Can improve upon words in cartoon	Can approximate words in cartoon	Can reproduce words in cartoon with minimal assistance	Cannot reproduce words in cartoon with minimal assistance
Mental model	Develops mental model that explains formula for slope of line that could be used as example for classroom	Develops mental model that explains formula for slope of line	Can develop mental model that explains formula for slope with minimal assistance	Cannot develop mental model that explains formula for slope of line with minimal assistance
Problem solving	Can change positions of people in hotel and create problems for others to solve	Can change positions of people in hotel and identify their new positions	Can change positions of people in hotel and identify their new positions with minimal assistance	Cannot change positions of people in hotel and identify their positions with minimal assistance

MENTAL MODEL—ALGEBRA

Standard: Algebra

Use multiple representations for situations to translate among diagrams, models, and symbolic expressions.

Explanation and Directions:

Solving Equations with One Variable Using Cups and Counters

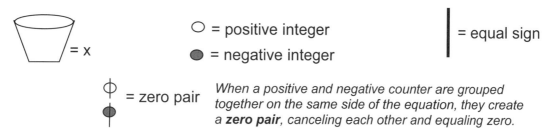

Using small cups with two-color counters, create the equation:

$$x + 3 = 7$$

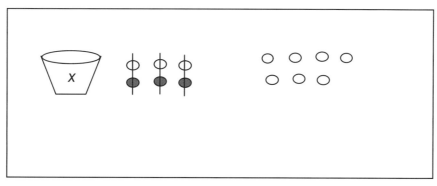

Isolate the variable x on one side by combining opposite counters on the x-side to make zero pairs.

Combine the same number of opposite counters to the counters on the other side of the equation.

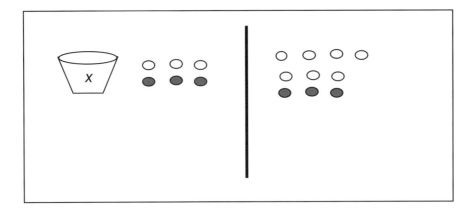

Cancel the zero pairs by removing them from the mat.

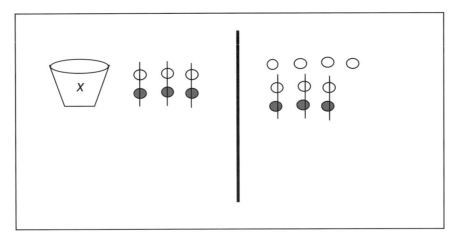

x = 4

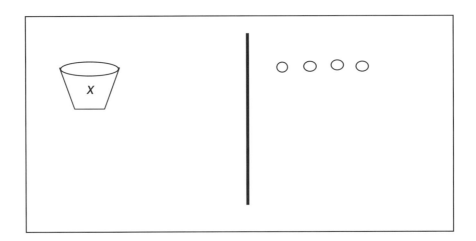

STEP SHEET

Standard: Algebra

Use multiple representations for situations to translate among diagrams, models, and symbolic expressions.

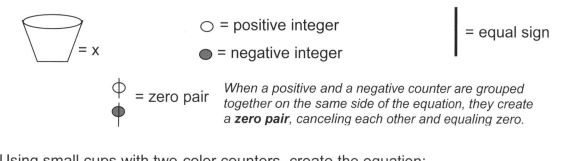

○ = positive integer

● = negative integer

| = equal sign

⌀ = zero pair

*When a positive and a negative counter are grouped together on the same side of the equation, they create a **zero pair**, canceling each other and equaling zero.*

Using small cups with two-color counters, create the equation:

x + 3 = 7

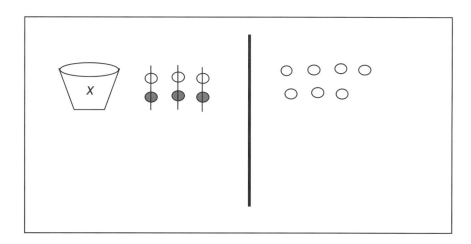

Isolate the variable x on one side by combining opposite counters on the x-side to make zero pairs.

Combine the same number of opposite counters to the counters on the other side of the equation.

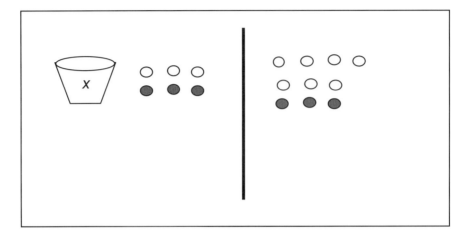

Cancel the zero pairs by removing them from the mat.

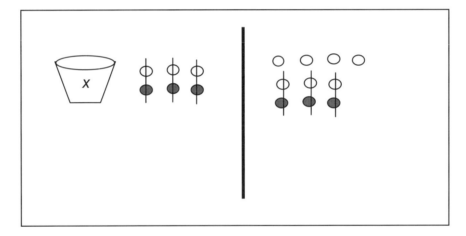

x = 4

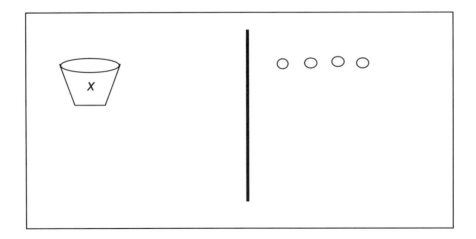

www.ahaprocess.com

Drawing

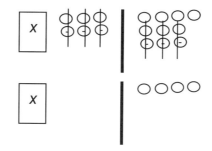

Steps:

1. Draw x as a rectangle.
2. Draw the constants using circles.
3. Isolate x by adding enough opposite circles to each side to make a zero pair on the x side.
4. Remove zero pairs on both sides.
5. Evaluate x.

Graph

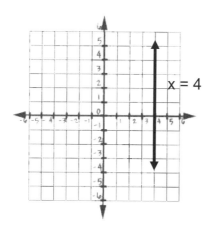

x = 4

Algebraic Solution

$$x + 3 = 7$$
$$- 3 \quad -3$$
$$\overline{}$$
$$x = 4$$

RUBRIC

Standard: Algebra

Use multiple representations for situations to translate among diagrams, models, and symbolic expressions.

Criteria	4 Exceeds Standard	3 Meets Standard	2 Is Below Standard	1 Does Not Meet Standard
Process	Uses more than two representations to solve equations	Follows each step of given process	Follows each step of process with assistance	Does not follow given process with minimal assistance
Computation	Verifies correct answer	Makes no errors	Makes no significant error(s)	Makes significant error(s)
Problem solving	Justifies process and solution	Determines reasonable-ness of solution	Uses appropriate process with assistance	Uses incorrect process
Mathematical language	Can explain process to others	Can explain process	Can explain parts of process	Cannot explain process

www.ahaprocess.com

Factoring Polynomials
Z-Box

$$x^2 - 3x - 4$$

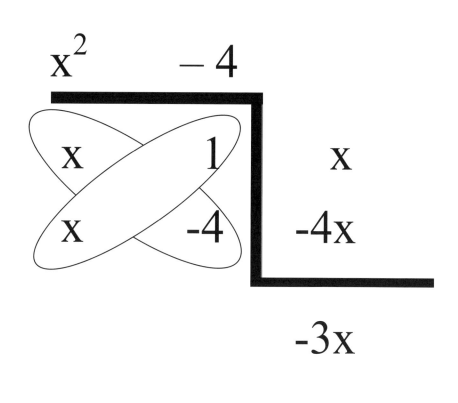

$$(x - 4)(x + 1)$$

MENTAL MODEL—ALGEBRA

Standard: Algebra

Represent and analyze mathematical situations and structures using algebraic symbols to express mathematical relationships using equations.

STEP SHEET

1. Write the Ax^2 and the C terms at the top of the "z."
2. Write the Bx term at the bottom of the "x."
3. Write the factors of Ax^2 and C inside the "z."
4. Cross-multiply and record the product outside the "z."
5. Add the products and compare with the Bx term.
6. Repeat, if necessary.

     www.ahaprocess.com

RUBRIC

Standard: Algebra

Represent and analyze mathematical situations and structures using algebraic symbols to express mathematical relationships using equations.

	4	3	2	1
Criteria	**Exceeds Standard**	**Meets Standard**	**Is Below Standard**	**Does Not Meet Standard**
Problem solving	Applies process appropriately to problems outside classwork	Applies process appropriately to problems in classwork	Applies process with minimal assistance	Cannot apply process with minimal assistance
Computation	Explains computations to others	Computes accurately	Computes accurately with minimal assistance	Cannot perform computations with minimal assistance
Process	Can explain process to others	Follows process correctly	Follows process with minimal assistance	Cannot follow process with minimal assistance

CHAPTER THREE
Geometry

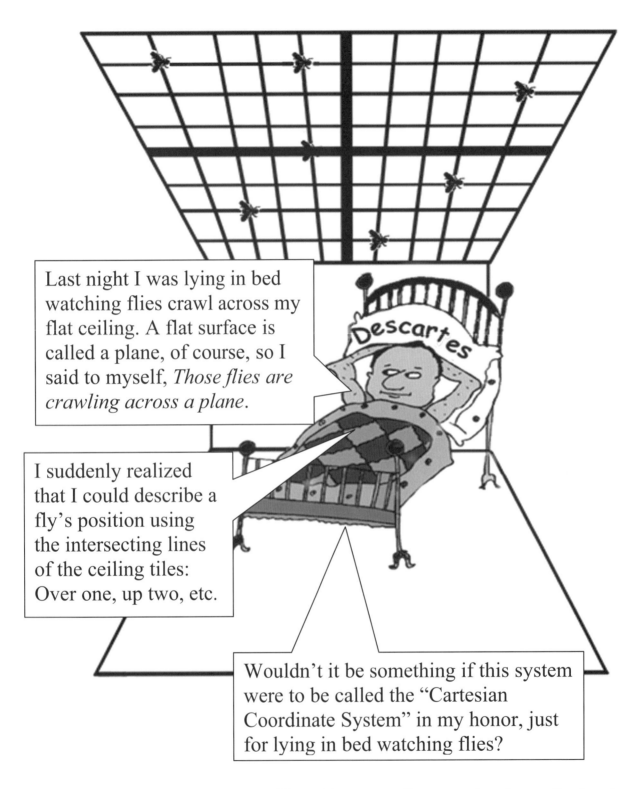

The word Cartesian means "from Descartes," so people often talk about the Cartesian Plane when they are using this system.

www.ahaprocess.com

MENTAL MODEL—GEOMETRY

Standard: Geometry

Specify locations and describe spatial relationships using coordinate geometry and other representational systems.

Use Cartesian coordinates and other coordinate systems—such as navigational, polar, or spherical systems—to analyze geometric situations.

Explanation of Mental Model:

This "poster style" mental model is designed for frequent viewing.

STEP SHEET

1. Study the mental model.
2. Write a definition of "Cartesian" in your own words.
3. Compare your definition with a dictionary definition.
4. Read about Descartes.
5. Decide if you believe the story about how he had the idea about coordinate planes.
6. Write another story about a different way that Descartes might have had this idea.
7. Play Battleship with a friend.
8. Describe how the game Battleship is similar to Descartes' discovery.

RUBRIC

Standard: Geometry

Specify locations and describe spatial relationships using coordinate geometry and other representational systems.

Use Cartesian coordinates and other coordinate systems—such as navigational, polar, or spherical systems—to analyze geometric situations.

Criteria	4 Exceeds Standard	3 Meets Standard	2 Is Below Standard	1 Does Not Meet Standard
Process	Can explain relationship between Battleship and Cartesian Plane to others	Can accurately explain relationship between Battleship and Cartesian Plane	Can explain relationship between Battleship and Cartesian Plane with minimal assistance	Cannot explain relationship between Battleship and Cartesian Plane with minimal assistance
Mathematical language	Writes definition of "Cartesian" that could be used as example for classroom	Writes correct definition of "Cartesian"	Writes definition of "Cartesian" with minimal assistance	Cannot write accurate definition of "Cartesian" with minimal assistance
Mental model	Develops storyline mental model that could be used as example for classroom	Develops accurate personal storyline mental model	Develops storyline mental model with minimal assistance	Cannot develop accurate storyline mental model with minimal assistance
Computation	Applies theory of Cartesian Plane in other disciplines	Can apply theory of Cartesian Plane in classwork	Can apply theory of Cartesian Plane with minimal assistance	Cannot accurately apply theory of Cartesian Plane with minimal assistance

www.ahaprocess.com

Geometry: Chords, Tangents, Diameter

First student: When is a line in agreement with a circle?

Second student: When it is in accord (in a chord). Ha ha!

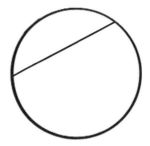

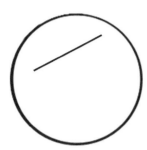

First student: When is a line not in a chord (in accord) with a circle?

Second student: When it does not stay in touch.

First student: When is a line not a chord?

Second student: When it goes off on a tangent.

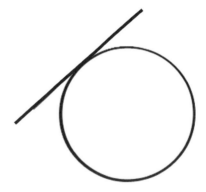

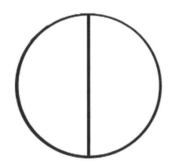

First student: What do we call a chord that seeks attention?

Second student: A diameter. It's always in the center of things.

Note: A chord is a segment whose end points lie on a given circle.

MENTAL MODEL—GEOMETRY

Standard: Geometry

Analyze characteristics and properties of two- and three-dimensional geometric shapes and develop mathematical arguments about geometric relationships.

Understand relationships among the angles, side lengths, perimeters, areas, and volumes of similar objects.

STEP SHEET

1. Study the mental model.
2. Write definitions of the terms chord, tangent, and diameter in your own words.
3. Compare your definitions with glossary definitions.
4. Modify your definitions as necessary, then illustrate them.
5. Write and illustrate additional riddles using these and other geometric terms.

RUBRIC

Standard: Geometry

Analyze characteristics and properties of two- and three-dimensional geometric shapes and develop mathematical arguments about geometric relationships.

Understand relationships among the angles, side lengths, perimeters, areas, and volumes of similar objects.

Criteria	4 Exceeds Standard	3 Meets Standard	2 Is Below Standard	1 Does Not Meet Standard
Application	Applies concepts to new situations independently	Applies concepts to new situations in classwork	Applies concepts to new situations with minimal assistance	Cannot apply concepts to new situations with minimal assistance
Mathematical language	Recognizes and explains related terms	Gives in-depth explanation of terms	Uses correct terms with some assistance	Uses terms incorrectly
Mental model	Writes riddles that could be used as examples for classroom	Writes riddles that serve as appropriate personal mental model	Can define terms but cannot write accurate riddle	Cannot define terms for use in riddle

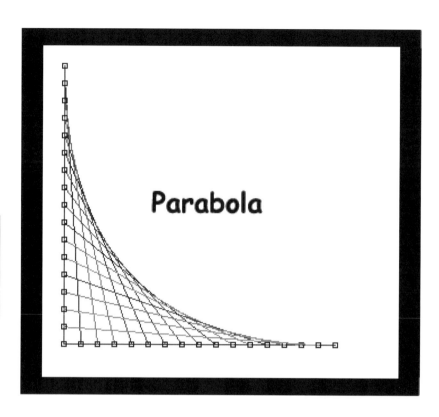

Parabola

String Art

String art was first created by Charlotte Agnes Scott. In 1894 Scott's book, titled *An Introductory Account of Certain Modern Ideas and Methods in Plane Analytical Geometry,* was published. It is still widely used.

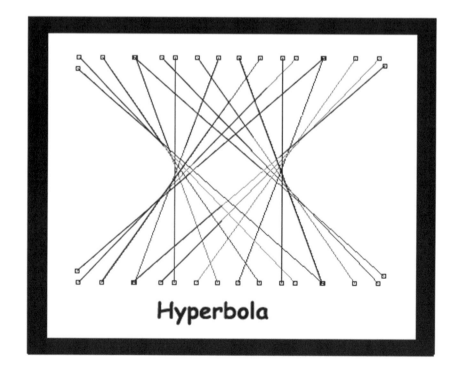

Hyperbola

MENTAL MODEL—GEOMETRY

Standard: Geometry

Use visualization, spatial reasoning, and geometric modeling to solve problems.

Recognize and apply geometric ideas and relationships in areas outside the mathematics classroom, such as art, science, and everyday life.

Explanation of Mental Model:

This "poster style" mental model is designed for frequent viewing and to spark a discussion of geometric ideas outside the mathematics classroom.

STEP SHEET

1. Read about string art.
2. Find examples in books of string art that look similar to the parabolas and hyperbolas on the poster.
3. Find examples of string art that look like other geometric shapes.
4. Find additional examples of geometry in everyday life.
5. Design a personal mental model that illustrates parabolas, hyperbolas, and other geometric shapes.

RUBRIC

Standard: Geometry

Use visualization, spatial reasoning, and geometric modeling to solve problems.

Recognize and apply geometric ideas and relationships in areas outside the mathematics classroom, such as art, science, and everyday life.

	4	3	2	1
Criteria	**Exceeds Standard**	**Meets Standard**	**Is Below Standard**	**Does Not Meet Standard**
Mental model	Designs mental model that could be used as example for classroom	Develops accurate mental model	Develops mental model with minimal assistance	Cannot develop mental model with minimal assistance
Mathematical language	Can create and evaluate geometric relationships from outside classwork	Recognizes some geometric relationships from outside classwork	Can select geometric shapes from outside classwork from list of options	Cannot select geometric shapes from outside classwork from list of options

www.ahaprocess.com

Pythagorean Theorem: $a^2 + b^2 = c^2$

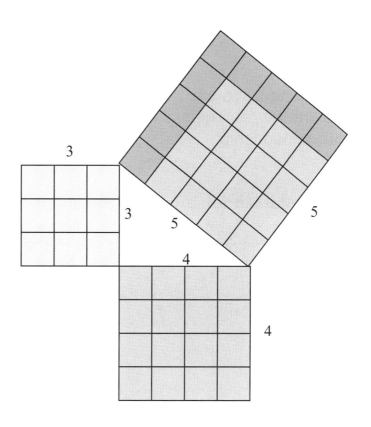

$$a^2 + b^2 = c^2$$

$$3^2 + 4^2 = 5^2$$

$$9 + 16 = 25$$

$$25 = 25$$

Square of one side + Square of other side = Square of hypotenuse

MENTAL MODEL—GEOMETRY

Standard: Geometry

Analyze characteristics and properties of two- and three-dimensional geometric shapes and develop mathematical arguments about geometric relationships.

Create and critique inductive and deductive arguments concerning geometric ideas and relationships, such as congruence, similarity, and the Pythagorean relationship.

Explanation of Mental Model:

The mental model graphically explains why the Pythagorean Theorem is true.

STEP SHEET

I. Study Pythagorean Theorem

Determine the length of the hypotenuse of a right triangle with legs of 3 inches and 4 inches.

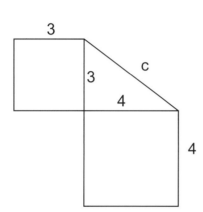

$$c^2 = a^2 + b^2$$

$$c^2 = 3^2 + 4^2$$

$$c^2 = 9 + 6$$

$$c^2 = 25$$

$$c = 5$$

1. Draw a right triangle using side measures of 5, 12, 13, or other Pythagorean triple.
2. Sketch a square on each side of the triangle.
3. Grid one-unit squares in each large square.
4. Verify that the area of the square on the hypotenuse is equal to the sum of the area of the squares on the other two sides.

II. Apply Pythagorean Theorem

1. Draw a right triangle and label with the given information.
2. Write the Pythagorean Theorem.
3. Substitute given values in the Pythagorean Theorem.
4. Solve the equation.

RUBRIC

Standard: Geometry

Analyze characteristics and properties of two- and three-dimensional geometric shapes and develop mathematical arguments about geometric relationships.

Create and critique inductive and deductive arguments concerning geometric ideas and relationships, such as congruence, similarity, and the Pythagorean relationship.

	4	3	2	1
Criteria	**Exceeds Standard**	**Meets Standard**	**Is Below Standard**	**Does Not Meet Standard**
Process	Solves numerous problems using Pythagorean Theorem	Solves problems using Pythagorean Theorem in classwork	Follows each step of given process with minimal assistance	Does not follow given process with minimal assistance
Computation	Can explain computations to others	Makes no errors	Makes few significant error(s)	Makes significant error(s)
Problem solving	Can apply method and solution outside classwork	Applies method and solution in classwork	Uses method and solution with minimal assistance	Cannot use method and solution independently with minimal assistance
Mathematical language	Recognizes and explains related topics	Gives in-depth explanation of labels	Uses labels correctly with some assistance	Uses labels incorrectly

MENTAL MODEL—GEOMETRY

Standard: Geometry

Analyze characteristics and properties of two- and three-dimensional geometric shapes and develop mathematical arguments about geometric relationships.

Precisely describe, classify, and understand relationships among types of two- and three-dimensional objects using their defining properties.

Explanation of Mental Model:

This "poster style" mental model is designed for frequent viewing.

STEP SHEET

1. Study the mental model.
2. Write definitions of *sector* and *arc* in your own words.
3. Compare your definitions with glossary definitions.
4. Find various sectors and arcs in your environment and estimate their degrees.
5. Design a personal mental model that illustrates the meanings of sector and arc.

RUBRIC

Standard: Geometry

Analyze characteristics and properties of two- and three-dimensional geometric shapes and develop mathematical arguments about geometric relationships.

Precisely describe, classify, and understand relationships among types of two- and three-dimensional objects using their defining properties.

Criteria	4 Exceeds Standard	3 Meets Standard	2 Is Below Standard	1 Does Not Meet Standard
Mental model	Develops mental model that could be used as example for classroom	Develops appropriate personal mental model	Develops mental-model poster with minimal assistance	Cannot develop accurate mental model with minimal assistance
Mathematical language	Recognizes and explains related topics	Gives in-depth explanation of labels	Uses correct labels inconsistently	Does not use labels correctly
Problem solving	Accurately estimates degrees of sectors in environment	Estimates degrees of sectors in environment within 15 degrees	Estimates degrees of sectors in environment within 25 degrees	Cannot estimate degrees of sectors in environment within 25 degrees

Walk Straight!
with
Supplementary
Vitamins

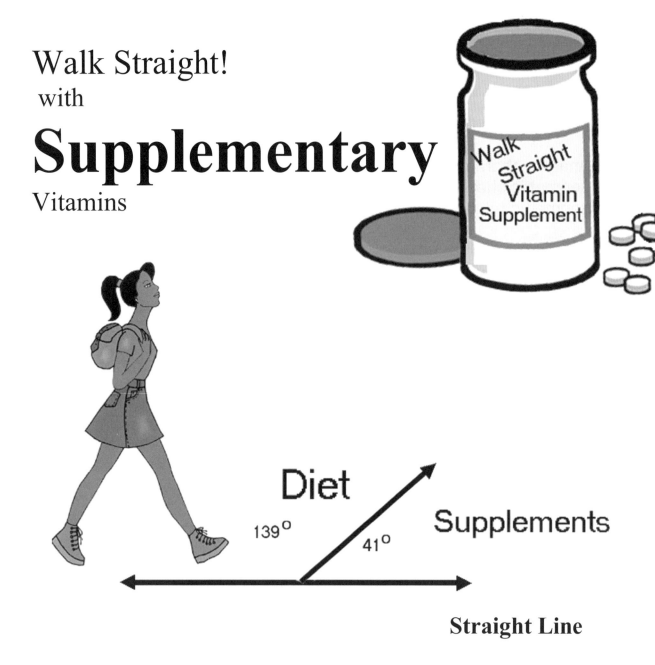

Diet

139°

41°

Supplements

Straight Line

Diet + Supplementary Vitamins = 180°,

a Straight Line!

Two angles are called supplementary angles if the sum of their degree measurements equals 180 degrees. One of the supplementary angles is called the supplement of the other.

www.ahaprocess.com

MENTAL MODEL—GEOMETRY

Standard: Geometry

Analyze characteristics and properties of two- and three-dimensional geometric shapes and develop mathematical arguments about geometric relationships.

Understand relationships among the angles, side lengths, perimeters, areas, and volumes of similar objects.

Explanation of Mental Model:

This "poster style" mental model is designed for frequent viewing.

STEP SHEET

1. Study the mental model.
2. Write in your own words a definition of *supplementary angles*.
3. Compare your definition with glossary definitions.
4. Find examples of supplementary angles in your environment.
5. On a sheet of paper draw various supplementary angles. Measure and write the number of degrees in the first angle. Ask a friend to compute the number of degrees in the supplementary angle.
6. Design a mental model than illustrates supplementary angles.

RUBRIC

Standard: Geometry

Analyze characteristics and properties of two- and three-dimensional geometric shapes and develop mathematical arguments about geometric relationships.

Understand relationships among the angles, side lengths, perimeters, areas, and volumes of similar objects.

Criteria	4 **Exceeds Standard**	3 **Meets Standard**	2 **Is Below Standard**	1 **Does Not Meet Standard**
Process	Measures and draws various angles for friends to compute	Draws at least five angles for friends to compute	Draws angles for friends to compute with minimal assistance	Cannot draw angles for friends to compute with minimal assistance
Mathematical language	Writes definition that could be used as example for classroom	Writes accurate definition	Writes accurate definition with minimal assistance	Cannot write accurate definition with minimal assistance
Mental model	Designs mental model that could be used as example for classroom	Designs appropriate personal mental model	Designs mental model with minimal assistance	Cannot design mental model with minimal assistance

Criteria	4 — Exceeds Standard	3 — Meets Standard	2 — Is Below Standard	1 — Does Not Meet Standard
Computation	Can assist others in drawing and computing supplementary angles	Accurately computes supplementary angles on friends' papers	Can compute supplementary angles on friends' papers with minimal assistance	Cannot compute supplementary angles on friends' papers with minimal assistance
Problem solving	Identifies multiple supplementary angles in environment	Identifies at least five supplementary angles in environment	Can find supplementary angles in environment with minimal assistance	Cannot identify supplementary angles in environment with minimal assistance

CHAPTER FOUR
Measurement

Area of a Circle

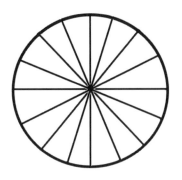

Many years ago a man named Archimedes probably sliced a pizza into thin slices …

Then he probably lined the slices up to form a rectangular shape.

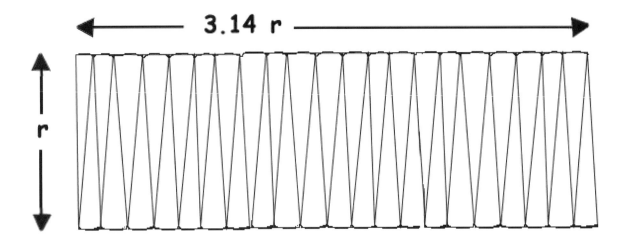

Then he probably discovered that the length of the rectangle is 3.14 times the width (the radius of the circle). He knew that this number (3.14) must be special, so he called it π (pi).

Finally, Archimedes found the area of the rectangle the way his teacher had taught him, by multiplying the length times the width:

$$\pi\, r \times r = \pi\, r^2$$

This is the formula for the area of a circle.

MENTAL MODEL—MEASUREMENT

Standard: Measurement

Analyze characteristics and properties of two- and three-dimensional geometric shapes and develop mathematical arguments about geometric relationships.

Understand relationships among the angles, side lengths, perimeters, areas, and volumes of similar objects.

Explanation of Mental Model:

This mental model can help students to develop a concrete understanding of the formula for the area of a circle.

STEP SHEET

1. Write your own definitions of *area* and *radius*.
2. Compare your definitions with glossary definitions.
3. Cut a circle out of paper. Draw the radius of the circle.
4. Cut the circle into multiple sectors and line them up, as illustrated, into a rectangular shape.
5. Measure the length and the width of the rectangle. The length should be approximately 3.14 times the radius of the original circle.
6. Write your own definition of pi.
7. Compare your definition with a glossary definition.
8. Study the mental model. Write a paragraph explaining the formula for the area of a rectangle.
9. Write a paragraph explaining the formula for the area of a circle (πr^2).
10. Design a mental model that explains the formula for the area of a circle.

RUBRIC

Standard: Measurement

Analyze characteristics and properties of two- and three-dimensional geometric shapes and develop mathematical arguments about geometric relationships.

Understand relationships among the angles, side lengths, perimeters, areas, and volumes of similar objects.

	4	3	2	1
Criteria	**Exceeds Standard**	**Meets Standard**	**Is Below Standard**	**Does Not Meet Standard**
Process	Can reproduce circle diagram and explain to others	Can reproduce circle diagram	Can reproduce circle diagram with minimal assistance	Cannot reproduce circle diagram with minimal assistance
Computation	Can explain to others how to compute area of circle	Can compute area of circle	Can compute area of circle with minimal assistance	Cannot compute area of circle with minimal assistance
Problem solving	Can apply formula to new situations outside classwork	Can apply formula to new situations in classwork	Can apply formula to new situations with minimal assistance	Cannot apply formula to new situations with minimal assistance

www.ahaprocess.com

Criteria	4 Exceeds Standard	3 Meets Standard	2 Is Below Standard	1 Does Not Meet Standard
Mathematical language (1)	Writes definitions of terms that could be used as example for classroom	Writes accurate definitions of terms	Writes definitions of terms with minimal assistance	Cannot write definitions of terms with minimal assistance
Mathematical language (2)	Writes paragraph explaining formula for area of circle that could be used as example for classroom	Writes paragraph accurately explaining formula for area of circle	Writes paragraph explaining formula for area of circle with minimal assistance	Cannot write paragraph explaining formula for area of circle with minimal assistance
Mental model	Develops mental model that could be used as example for classroom	Develops appropriate personal mental model	Develops accurate mental model with minimal assistance	Cannot develop accurate mental model with minimal assistance

Area of a Cylinder

A cylinder is dozens or hundreds of congruent circles stacked up.

If the area of one of the circles is πr^2,

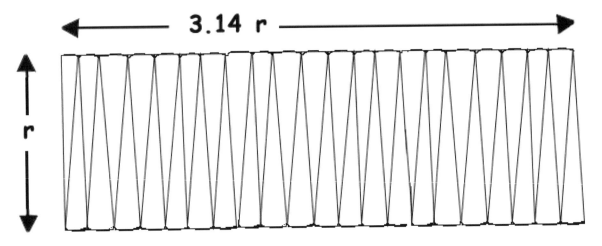

and if h is the height of the cylinder,

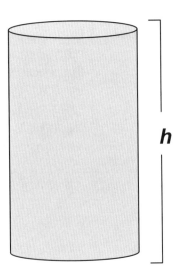

then the volume of the cylinder is $\pi r^2 h$.

MENTAL MODEL—MEASUREMENT

Standard: Measurement

Apply appropriate techniques, tools, and formulas to determine measurements.

Develop strategies to determine the surface area and volume of selected prisms, pyramids, and cylinders.

Explanation of Mental Model:

This mental model builds concrete understanding of the formula for the area of a cylinder.

STEP SHEET

1. Write the definitions of *area* and *radius* in your own words.
2. Compare your definitions with glossary definitions.
3. Study the mental model explaining the formula for the area of a cylinder.
4. Write your own definition of *cylinder*.
5. Write a paragraph explaining the formula for the area of a cylinder. (Add height to the formula πr^2 to establish the formula for the area of a cylinder: $\pi r^2 h$.)
6. Design a mental model explaining the formula for the area of a cylinder.

RUBRIC

Standard: Measurement

Analyze characteristics and properties of two- and three-dimensional geometric shapes and develop mathematical arguments about geometric relationships.

Understand relationships among the angles, side lengths, perimeters, areas, and volumes of similar objects.

Criteria	4 Exceeds Standard	3 Meets Standard	2 Is Below Standard	1 Does Not Meet Standard
Mental model	Develops mental model that could be used as example for classroom	Develops appropriate personal mental model	Develops mental model with minimal assistance	Cannot develop accurate mental model with minimal assistance
Computation	Can assist others in computing area of cylinder	Can compute area of cylinder	Can compute area of cylinder with minimal assistance	Cannot compute area of cylinder with minimal assistance
Problem solving	Can apply formula to new situations outside classwork	Can apply formula to new situations in classwork	Can apply formula to new situations with minimal assistance	Cannot apply formula to new situations with minimal assistance

Criteria	4 Exceeds Standard	3 Meets Standard	2 Is Below Standard	1 Does Not Meet Standard
Mathematical language (1)	Writes definitions of terms that could be used as example for classroom	Writes accurate definitions of terms	Writes definitions of terms with minimal assistance	Cannot write definitions of terms with minimal assistance
Mathematical language (2)	Writes paragraph explaining formula for area of cylinder that could be used as example for classroom	Writes paragraph accurately explaining formula for area of cylinder	Writes paragraph explaining formula for area of cylinder with minimal assistance	Cannot write paragraph explaining formula for area of cylinder with minimal assistance

The volume of a cone is 1/3 the volume of a cylinder with equal height and radius:

Area of Cone: $1/3\ \pi r^2 h$

www.ahaprocess.com

MENTAL MODEL—MEASUREMENT

Standard: Measurement

Apply appropriate techniques, tools, and formulas to determine measurements.

Develop and use formulas to determine the circumference of circles and the area of triangles, parallelograms, trapezoids, and circles, and develop strategies to find the area of more complex shapes.

STEP SHEET

1. Study the mental model.
2. Study the following example comparing the volume of a cone with the volume of a cylinder with a radius of 2 units and a height of 4 units:

$$\text{Volume of cone} = \frac{1}{3}\pi r^2 h \qquad\qquad \text{Volume of cylinder} = \pi r^2 h$$

$$\text{Volume of cone} = \frac{1}{3}(3.14)(2^2)(4) \qquad\qquad \text{Volume of cylinder} = (3.14)(2^2)(4)$$

$$\text{Volume of cone} = \frac{1}{3}(3.14)(4)(4) \qquad\qquad \text{Volume of cylinder} = (3.14)(4)(4)$$

$$\text{Volume of cone} = \frac{1}{3}(3.14)(16) \qquad\qquad \text{Volume of cylinder} = (3.14)(16)$$

$$\text{Volume of cone} = \frac{3.14}{3}(16) \qquad\qquad \text{Volume of cylinder} \approx 48 \text{ units}^3$$

$$\text{Volume of cone} \approx 16 \text{ units}^3$$

3. Draw a chart with three columns. Write *circle* at the top of the first column, *cylinder* at the top of the second column, and *cone* at the top of the third column.
4. In each column write the appropriate formula.
5. Beneath the formula write a one-sentence explanation of the formula.
6. Draw a mental model that explains the formula for the area of a cone.

RUBRIC

Standard: Measurement

Apply appropriate techniques, tools, and formulas to determine measurements.

Develop and use formulas to determine the circumference of circles and the area of triangles, parallelograms, trapezoids, and circles, and develop strategies to find the area of more complex shapes.

Criteria	4 Exceeds Standard	3 Meets Standard	2 Is Below Standard	1 Does Not Meet Standard
Mental model	Develops mental model that could be used as example for classroom	Develops appropriate personal mental model	Develops mental model with minimal assistance	Cannot develop accurate mental model with minimal assistance
Computation	Can assist others in computing area of cone	Can compute area of cone	Can compute area of cone with minimal assistance	Cannot compute area of cone with minimal assistance
Problem solving	Can apply formula to new situations outside classwork	Can apply formula to new situations in classwork	Can apply formula to new situations with minimal assistance	Cannot apply formula to new situations

  www.ahaprocess.com

Criteria	4 Exceeds Standard	3 Meets Standard	2 Is Below Standard	1 Does Not Meet Standard
Mathematical language (1)	Draws chart that could be used as example for classroom	Draws accurate chart	Draws chart with minimal assistance	Cannot draw accurate chart with minimal assistance
Mathematical language (2)	Writes sentences explaining formulas for three shapes that could be used as example for classroom	Writes sentences accurately explaining formula for each of three shapes	Writes sentences explaining formula for each of three shapes with minimal assistance	Cannot write sentences explaining formula for three shapes with minimal assistance

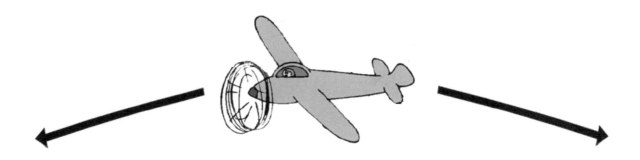

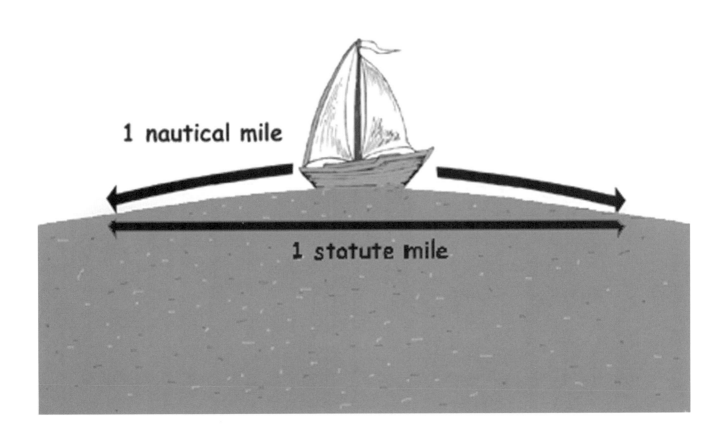

1 nautical mile

1 statute mile

www.ahaprocess.com

MENTAL MODEL—MEASUREMENT

Standard: Measurement

Understand measurable attributes of objects and the units, systems, and processes of measurement.

Understand relationships among units and convert from one unit to another within the same system.

Understand both metric and customary systems of measurement.

Explanation of Mental Model:

This "poster style" mental model is designed for frequent viewing.

STEP SHEET

1. Study the mental model.
2. Write definitions of *nautical* and *statute* mile in your own words.
3. Compare your definitions with the notes below:
   - A nautical mile is based on the circumference of the planet Earth. This unit of measurement is used by all nations for air and sea travel.
   - If you are traveling at 1 nautical mile per hour, you are traveling at a speed of 1 knot.
   - A nautical mile is 6,076 feet. A statute mile is 5,280 feet.
4. List at least three uses of each measurement.
5. Write word problems requiring conversion between the two measurement systems for your friends to solve. Your word problems should follow these rules:
   a. Your word problem must be a question.
   b. You must have four possible answers, only one of which can be correct.
   c. One of your incorrect choices must be funny.
   d. None of your choices can be "none of the above" or "all of the above."
6. Design a mental model that explains nautical and statute miles.

RUBRIC

Standard: Measurement

Understand measurable attributes of objects and the units, systems, and processes of measurement.

Understand relationships among units and convert from one unit to another within the same system.

Understand both metric and customary systems of measurement.

Criteria	4 Exceeds Standard	3 Meets Standard	2 Is Below Standard	1 Does Not Meet Standard
Mental model	Develops mental model that could be used as example for classroom	Develops appropriate personal mental model	Develops mental model with minimal assistance	Cannot develop accurate mental model with minimal assistance
Computation (1)	Can assist others with conversions from nautical to statute mile	Can convert from nautical to statute mile	Can convert from nautical to statute mile with minimal assistance	Cannot convert from nautical to statute mile with minimal assistance
Computation (2)	Can answer and critique questions written by peers	Can answer questions written by peers	Can answer questions written by peers with minimal assistance	Cannot answer questions written by peers with minimal assistance

Criteria	4 **Exceeds Standard**	3 **Meets Standard**	2 **Is Below Standard**	1 **Does Not Meet Standard**
Mathematical language (1)	Writes definitions of terms that could be used as example for classroom	Writes accurate definitions of terms	Writes definitions of terms with minimal assistance	Cannot write definitions of terms with minimal assistance
Mathematical language (2)	Writes questions that could be used on test	Writes accurate questions	Writes accurate questions with minimal assistance	Cannot write accurate questions with minimal assistance

Gallon Guy

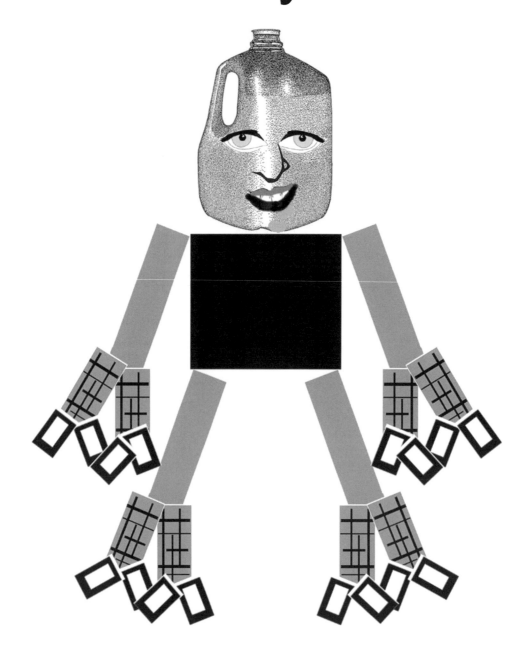

www.ahaprocess.com

MENTAL MODEL—MEASUREMENT

Standard: Measurement

Understand measurable attributes of objects and the units, systems, and processes of measurement.

Explanation of Mental Model:

This "poster style" mental model is designed for frequent viewing.

STEP SHEET

1. Study the mental model.
2. Construct your own Gallon Guy using four sheets of paper, all the same size.
3. One piece of paper is his body. It represents one gallon.
4. Cut the second sheet of paper into four equal parts lengthwise. These pieces become his upper arms and legs and represent four quarts in a gallon.
5. Cut the third sheet of paper into eight equal pieces. These pieces become his lower arms and legs and represent pints.
6. Cut the fourth sheet of paper into 16 equal pieces. These pieces become his fingers and toes and represent cups. (Gallon Guy has no thumbs and no big toes.)
7. Write problems that require conversion from gallons to quarts, pints, or cups.
8. Design another mental model that demonstrates the relationships of gallons, quarts, pints, and cups.

RUBRIC

Standard: Measurement

Understand measurable attributes of objects and the units, systems, and processes of measurement.

Criteria	4 Exceeds Standard	3 Meets Standard	2 Is Below Standard	1 Does Not Meet Standard
Mental model	Develops mental-model poster that could be used as example for classroom	Develops appropriate personal mental-model poster	Develops mental-model poster with minimal assistance	Cannot develop accurate mental-model poster with minimal assistance
Computation (1)	Can assist others with conversions from gallons to quarts, pints, and cups	Can convert from gallons to quarts, pints, and cups	Can convert from gallons to quarts, pints, and cups with minimal assistance	Cannot convert from gallons to quarts, pints, and cups with minimal assistance
Computation (2)	Can assist others in constructing Gallon Guy	Can construct Gallon Guy	Can construct Gallon Guy with minimal assistance	Cannot construct Gallon Guy with minimal assistance

www.ahaprocess.com

CHAPTER FIVE
Problem Solving

Order of Operations (Multiplication and Addition)

In the problem 1 + 2 × 2, which operation should be performed first? Addition or multiplication?

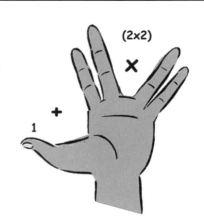

I have five fingers on my hand:
One single finger (1) plus two groups of two (2 × 2)

$$1 + 2 \times 2$$

What should I do first, add or multiply?

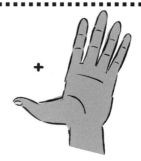

If I multiply first: $1 + 2 \times 2 =$

$1 + 4 = 5$ fingers

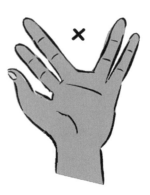

But, if I add first: $1 + 2 \times 2 =$

$3 \times 2 = 6$

Six fingers??!!

Answer: Multiplication (and division) should be performed before addition (or subtraction).

Hint: You can show people which operation you want them to perform first by drawing parentheses around that step: 1 + (2 x 2) = 5

MENTAL MODEL—PROBLEM SOLVING

Standard: Problem Solving

Students will:
- Build new mathematical knowledge through problem solving.
- Solve problems that arise in mathematics and other contexts.
- Apply and adapt a variety of appropriate strategies to solve problems.
- Monitor and reflect on the process of mathematical problem solving.

Explanation of Mental Model:

This "poster style" mental model is designed for frequent viewing.

STEP SHEET

1. Study the mental model.
2. Explain the order of operations to a friend by drawing an addition and a multiplication sign on a sheet of paper, then placing your fingers around the signs as illustrated. Illustrate each part of the mental model.
3. Solve several simple problems to repeat the proof of this step in the order of operations.
4. Design another mental model that illustrates this step and other steps in the order of operations.

RUBRIC

Standard: Problem Solving

Students will:
- Build new mathematical knowledge through problem solving.
- Solve problems that arise in mathematics and other contexts.
- Apply and adapt a variety of appropriate strategies to solve problems.
- Monitor and reflect on the process of mathematical problem solving.

Criteria	4 Exceeds Standard	3 Meets Standard	2 Is Below Standard	1 Does Not Meet Standard
Mental model	Develops mental model that could be used as example for classroom	Develops appropriate personal mental model	Develops mental model with minimal assistance	Cannot develop accurate mental model with minimal assistance
Computation	Can prove each step of order of operations	Can prove this step of order of operations	Can prove this step of order of operations with minimal assistance	Cannot prove this step of order of operations with minimal assistance
Problem solving (1)	Can apply proof of order of operations to new situations outside classwork	Can apply proof of order of operations to new situations in classwork	Can apply proof of order of operations with minimal assistance	Cannot apply proof of order of operations to new situations with minimal assistance

	4	3	2	1
Criteria	**Exceeds Standard**	**Meets Standard**	**Is Below Standard**	**Does Not Meet Standard**
Mathematical language	Can explain order of operations to others	Can give explanation of order of operations	Can explain order of operations with minimal assistance	Cannot explain order of operations with minimal assistance
Problem solving (2)	Applies proof to new data outside classwork	Applies proof to new data in classwork	Applies proof to new data with minimal assistance	Cannot apply proof to new data with minimal assistance

QDPAC

LETTER	WORD / SYMBOL	TEACHER DIRECTIONS	SENTENCE STARTER (use these to help students write about the math process)
Q	QUESTION ? ⌃___○	Find the stated or implied question. Underline the question, using a sentence frame.	I was asked to ...
D	DATA ___	<u>Underline</u> the important data in the problem. Cross out unnecessary information in the problem.	I knew ...
P	PLAN + − • ÷	Decide on the plan to follow: Operation or Other. Examine answers to see if there are any that can be eliminated. Cross them out.	I used ...
A	ANSWER ⬭	Show work. For multiple choice, circle the answer and the letter of the correct answer. Write it in the margin.	I found ...
C	CHECK ✓	Rework the problem. Work the problem backwards. Does it answer the question that was asked? ATQA	The answer is ... because ... Write a complete sentence that reflects the question using the answer. CSRQ: Complete sentence reflects question.

Adapted from Addison-Wesley Math

QDPAC Example:

Malcolm and his cousin wanted to buy a new music CD. They checked prices at five different stores. The first store they visited had the CD priced at $13.00, the second store at $13.50, the third store at $13.99, the fourth store at $14.99, and the fifth store had the CD priced at $7.00. ~~What~~ was the median price of the CD?

middle

~~A.~~ ~~$7.00~~

~~B.~~ ~~$12.50~~

(C.) $13.50

~~D.~~ ~~$14.99~~

$ ~~7.00~~

$ ~~13.00~~

($13.50)

$ ~~13.99~~

$ ~~14.99~~

Q
D
P
A
C

MENTAL MODEL—PROBLEM SOLVING

Standard: Problem Solving

Students will:
- Build new mathematical knowledge through problem solving.
- Solve problems that arise in mathematics and other contexts.
- Apply and adapt a variety of appropriate strategies to solve problems.
- Monitor and reflect on the process of mathematical problem solving.

STEP SHEET

1. Study the QDPAC steps.
2. Study the example above.
3. Write a math problem for a friend to solve using the QDPAC steps.
4. Check your friend's work.

RUBRIC

Standard: Problem Solving

Students will:
- Apply and adapt a variety of appropriate strategies to solve problems.
- Monitor and reflect on the process of mathematical problem solving.

Criteria	4 Exceeds Standard	3 Meets Standard	2 Is Below Standard	1 Does Not Meet Standard
Process	Can assist others in following QDPAC process	Accurately follows QDPAC process	Follows QDPAC process with minimal assistance	Cannot follow QDPAC process accurately with minimal assistance
Problem solving	Can assist others in solving problems using QDPAC steps	Accurately solves problems using QDPAC steps	Accurately solves problems using QDPAC steps with minimal assistance	Cannot accurately solve problems using QDPAC steps with minimal assistance

Distance = Rate times Time

d=rt

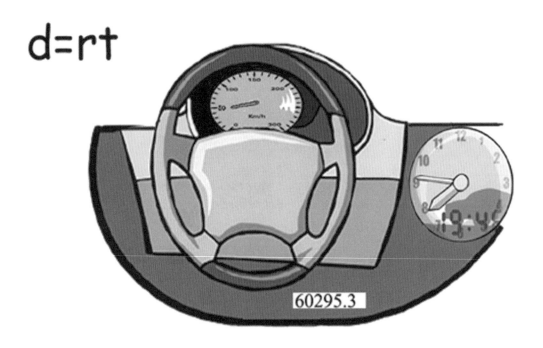

60295.3

Two hours (time) at 50 mph (rate)

= 100 miles (distance)

Note: The distance formula is an example of a proportionality problem:

$$\frac{x \; miles}{2 \; hours} = \frac{50 \; miles}{1 \; hour}$$

www.ahaprocess.com

MENTAL MODEL—PROBLEM SOLVING

Standard: Problem Solving

Students will:
- Build new mathematical knowledge through problem solving.
- Solve problems that arise in mathematics and other contexts.
- Apply and adapt a variety of appropriate strategies to solve problems.
- Monitor and reflect on the process of mathematical problem solving.

Explanation of Mental Model:

This "poster style" mental model is designed for frequent viewing.

STEP SHEET

1. Study the mental model.
2. Answer each of the following questions:
   - What item on the dashboard represents time?
   - What item on the dashboard represents distance?
   - What item on the dashboard represents rate?
3. Write word problems requiring the computation of distance (distance = rate times time), following these rules:
   - Your word problem must be in the form of a question.
   - You must provide four possible answers, only one of which can be correct.
   - One wrong answer must be funny.
   - You many not use "all of the above" or "none of the above."
4. Design a mental model illustrating d=rt.

RUBRIC

Standard: Problem Solving

Students will:
- Build new mathematical knowledge through problem solving.
- Solve problems that arise in mathematics and in other contexts.
- Apply and adapt a variety of appropriate strategies to solve problems.
- Monitor and reflect on the process of mathematical problem solving.

	4	**3**	**2**	**1**
Criteria	**Exceeds Standard**	**Meets Standard**	**Is Below Standard**	**Does Not Meet Standard**
Mental model	Develops mental model that could be used as example for classroom	Develops appropriate personal mental model	Develops mental model with minimal assistance	Cannot develop accurate mental model with minimal assistance
Computation	Can assist others in solving problems requiring formula d=rt	Can solve problems requiring formula d=rt	Can solve problems requiring formula d=rt with minimal assistance	Cannot solve problems requiring formula d=rt with minimal assistance
Problem solving (1)	Can apply formula d=rt to new situations outside classwork	Can apply formula d=rt to new situations in classwork	Can apply formula d=rt to new situations with minimal assistance	Cannot apply formula d=rt to new situations with minimal assistance
Problem solving (2)	Writes problems that could be included in test	Writes accurate word problems requiring formula d=rt	Writes word problems with minimal assistance	Cannot write word problems with minimal assistance

www.ahaprocess.com

Problem-Solving Process

Step 1: READ THE PROBLEM

Step 2: REREAD THE PROBLEM AND QUESTION

Step 3: MARK INFORMATION

Step 4: CHOOSE AN APPROPRIATE STRATEGY

Step 5: SOLVE

Step 6: IS THE QUESTION ANSWERED?

Move the clothespin down as you complete each step of the problem-solving process.

MENTAL MODEL—PROBLEM SOLVING

Standard: Problem Solving

Students will:

- Apply and adapt a variety of appropriate strategies to solve problems.
- Monitor and reflect on the process of mathematical problem solving.

Explanation of Mental Model:

Students can construct a Problem-Solving Process Step Sheet each six weeks.

STEP SHEET

1. Fold three sheets of paper at varying lengths so they overlap unevenly:

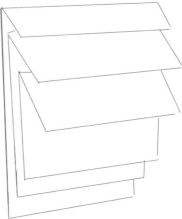

2. Write Step 1 on the top flap, Step 2 on the second flap, etc.

3. Underneath the Step 1 flap, write:
   Read the problem through completely to get a general idea of what the problem is asking.

4. Underneath the Step 2 flap, write:
   Reread to visualize the problem.
   Highlight or mark the question with a wavy line.

5. Underneath the Step 3 flap, write:
   Mark the important information and eliminate unnecessary information.

   Box the action/important words.

   CIRCLE needed information.

   Loop out extra information.

6. Underneath the Step 4 flap, write:
   Choose an operation (+ - X – ÷).
   Solve a simpler problem.
   Make an organized list.
   Look for a pattern.
   Use logical reasoning.
   Guess and check.
   Make a table.
   Use objects.
   Draw a picture.
   Act it out.
   Work backwards.

7. Underneath the Step 5 flap, write:
   Solve the problem.

8. Underneath the Step 6 flap, write:
   Read the question again.
   Does your solution answer the question?
   Does it make sense? Is it reasonable?
   Work the problem using a different strategy if possible.

9. When you use your Problem-Solving Process Step Sheet, move your clothespin down as you complete each step.

Source: Daily Math Skills Review *(2004) by Judy Sain*

RUBRIC

Standard: Problem Solving

Students will:
- Apply and adapt a variety of appropriate strategies to solve problems.
- Monitor and reflect on the process of mathematical problem solving.

Criteria	4 Exceeds Standard	3 Meets Standard	2 Is Below Standard	1 Does Not Meet Standard
Process	Can assist others in constructing Problem-Solving Step Sheet	Accurately constructs Problem-Solving Step Sheet	Constructs Problem-Solving Step Sheet with minimal assistance	Cannot accurately construct Problem-Solving Step Sheet with minimal assistance
Problem solving	Can assist others in solving math problems using Problem-Solving Step Sheet	Can solve math problems independently using Problem-Solving Step Sheet	Can solve math problems with minimal assistance using Problem-Solving Step Sheet	Cannot solve math problems using Problem-Solving Step Sheet with minimal assistance

www.ahaprocess.com

CHAPTER SIX

Data Analysis
and Probability

Reasoning
and Proof

Communication

Connections

Median (middle point) of all data

25, 37, 41, 44, 50, 56, 59, 67, 71, 74, 75, 82, 84, 88, 99

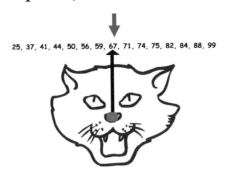

Median of lower part   Median of upper part

25, 37, 41, 44, 50, 56, 59, 67, 71, 74, 75, 82, 84, 88, 99

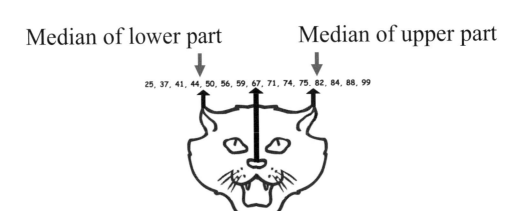

Box and Whisker Plot

25, 37, 41, 44, 50, 56, 59, 67, 71, 74, 75, 82, 84, 88, 99

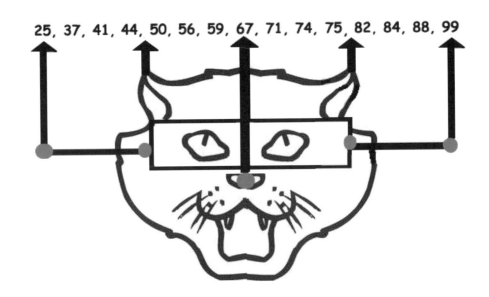

MENTAL MODEL—DATA ANALYSIS AND PROBABILITY

Standard: Data Analysis and Probability

Select and use appropriate statistical methods to analyze data, and understand and discuss the correspondence between data sets and their graphical representations, especially histograms, stem-and-leaf plots, box plots, and scatter plots.

Explanation of Mental Model:

This "poster style" mental model is designed for frequent viewing.

STEP SHEET

1. Study the mental model.
2. Write a definition of the word *median* in your own words.
3. Compare your definition with a glossary definition.
4. Write a paragraph explaining Box and Whisker Plots.
5. List three uses of a Box and Whisker Plot.
6. Collect or make up data and plot it in a Box and Whisker Plot.
7. Exchange plots with a peer and write a paragraph explaining the data in her or his Box and Whisker Plot.
8. Create a mental model that explains Box and Whisker Plots.

RUBRIC

Standard: Data Analysis and Probability

Select and use appropriate statistical methods to analyze data, understand and discuss the correspondence between data sets and their graphical representations, especially histograms, stem-and-leaf plots, box plots, and scatterplots.

Criteria	**4** **Exceeds Standard**	**3** **Meets Standard**	**2** **Is Below Standard**	**1** **Does Not Meet Standard**
Mental model	Develops mental-model poster that could be used as example for classroom	Develops appropriate personal mental-model poster	Develops mental-model poster with minimal assistance	Cannot develop accurate mental-model poster with minimal assistance
Computation	Can assist others in plotting data using Box and Whisker Plot	Can plot data using Box and Whisker Plot	Can plot data using Box and Whisker Plot with minimal assistance	Cannot plot data using Box and Whisker Plot with minimal assistance
Problem solving (1)	Can apply Box and Whisker Plot to new situations outside classwork	Can apply Box and Whisker Plot to new situations in classwork	Can apply Box and Whisker Plot to new situations with minimal assistance	Cannot apply Box and Whisker Plot to new situations with minimal assistance

Criteria	4 Exceeds Standard	3 Meets Standard	2 Is Below Standard	1 Does Not Meet Standard
Mathematical language (1)	Writes definitions of terms that could be used as example for classroom	Writes accurate definitions of terms	Writes definitions of terms with minimal assistance	Cannot write definitions of terms with minimal assistance
Mathematical language (2)	Writes paragraphs explaining Box and Whisker Plot that clarify concept to others	Writes paragraphs accurately explaining Box and Whisker Plot	Writes paragraphs accurately explaining Box and Whisker Plot with minimal assistance	Cannot write paragraph accurately explaining Box and Whisker Plot with minimal assistance
Problem solving (2)	Gathers and plots data on Box and Whisker Plot that could be used as example for classroom	Accurately gathers and plots data on Box and Whisker Plot	Gathers and plots data on Box and Whisker Plot with minimal assistance	Cannot gather and plot data on Box and Whisker Plot with minimal assistance

MENTAL MODEL—PROBABILITY

2	3	4	5	6	7	8	9	10	11	12

www.ahaprocess.com

MENTAL MODEL—DATA ANALYSIS AND PROBABILITY

Standard: Data Analysis and Probability

Understand and apply basic concepts of probability.

Explanation of Mental Model:

This mental model graphically demonstrates that some dice combinations have a higher probability than others.

STEP SHEET

1. Study the poster.
2. Write a paragraph explaining the concept of "Lucky Seven."
3. Roll a pair of dice 10 times and tally. Did the "Lucky Seven" probability hold true? Repeat 10 more times and total the two scores.
4. Develop a mental model explaining probability as related to rolling dice.
5. Make a chart showing the probability as related to tossing a coin 50 times.

RUBRIC

Standard: Data Analysis and Probability

Understand and apply basic concepts of probability.

Criteria	4 Exceeds Standard	3 Meets Standard	2 Is Below Standard	1 Does Not Meet Standard
Mental model	Develops mental-model poster that could be used as example for classroom	Develops accurate personal mental-model poster	Develops mental-model poster with minimal assistance	Cannot develop accurate mental-model poster with minimal assistance
Problem solving	Draws chart explaining coin-toss probability that could become class model	Draws chart accurately explaining coin-toss probability	Draws chart explaining coin-toss probability with minimal assistance	Cannot draw chart explaining coin-toss probability with minimal assistance
Mathematical language (1)	Writes definitions of terms that could be used as example for classroom	Writes accurate definitions of terms	Writes definitions of terms with minimal assistance	Cannot write definitions of terms with minimal assistance
Mathematical language (2)	Writes paragraph explaining "Lucky Seven" concept that clarifies the concept to others	Writes paragraph accurately explaining "Lucky Seven" concept	Writes paragraph explaining "Lucky Seven" concept with minimal assistance	Cannot write paragraph explaining "Lucky Seven" concept with minimal assistance

Conjunctions hold sentences together.

We played a good game, and we won.

Conjectures are ideas "thrown together."

(*con* = together; *jecture* = to throw)
Geometric Conjectures: *Conclusion, forming an opinion without proof.*

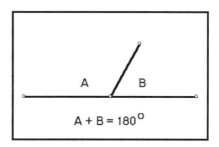

Linear Pair Conjecture: The measure of a straight angle is 180 degrees, so a linear pair of angles must add up to 180 degrees. (Linear pairs of angles add up to 180 degrees.)

Perpendicular Bisector of Chord Conjecture:
The perpendicular bisector of a chord in a circle passes through the center of the circle. (This could be a way to find the center of a circle.)

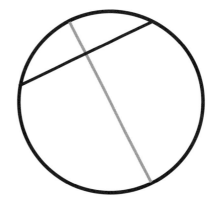

MENTAL MODEL—REASONING AND PROOF

Standard: Reasoning and Proof

Students will:
- Recognize reasoning and proof as fundamental aspects of mathematics.
- Make and investigate mathematical conjectures.

Explanation of Mental Model:

This "poster style" mental model is designed for establishing an understanding of conjectures.

STEP SHEET

1. Study the mental model.
2. Write a definition of the word *conjecture* in your own words.
3. Find at least three words that are derived from the same word base(s).
4. Rewrite the conjectures listed on the poster in your own words.
5. Find additional conjectures and write them in your own words.
6. Create a mental model that illustrates one or more of the conjectures.

RUBRIC

Standard: Reasoning and Proof

Students will:
- Recognize reasoning and proof as fundamental aspects of mathematics.
- Make and investigate mathematical conjectures.

Criteria	4 Exceeds Standard	3 Meets Standard	2 Is Below Standard	1 Does Not Meet Standard
Mental model	Develops mental-model poster that that could be used as example for classroom	Develops appropriate personal mental-model poster	Develops mental-model poster with minimal assistance	Cannot develop accurate mental-model poster with minimal assistance
Mathematical language (1)	Can write numerous conjectures in own words	Can rewrite conjectures on poster in own words	Can rewrite conjectures on poster in own words with minimal assistance	Cannot rewrite conjectures on poster in own words with minimal assistance
Problem solving	Can apply conjectures to real-life situations	Can apply conjectures to classwork problems	Can apply conjectures to classwork problems with minimal assistance	Cannot apply conjectures to classwork problems with minimal assistance
Mathematical language (2)	Can find numerous words that are derived from the same word base(s)	Can find at least three words that are derived from the same word base(s)	Can identify words that are derived from the same word base(s) with minimal assistance	Cannot identify words that are derived from the same word base(s) with minimal assistance

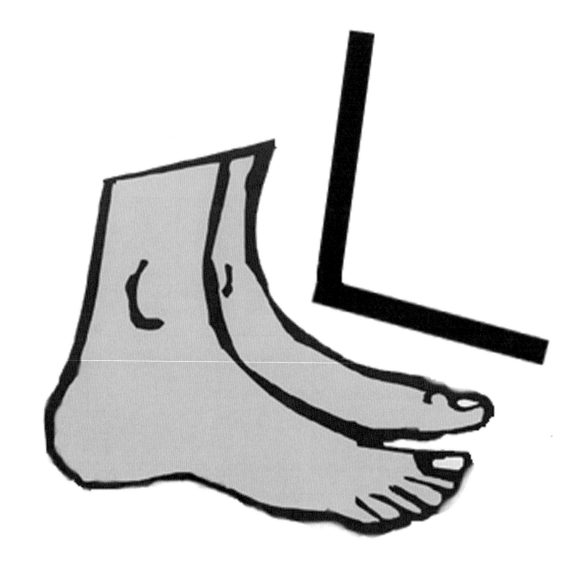

The words *ankle* and *angle* came from the same base word, meaning "a sharp bend."

MENTAL MODEL—COMMUNICATION

Standard: Communication

Students will:
- Communicate their mathematical thinking coherently and clearly to peers, teachers, and others.
- Use the language of mathematics to express mathematical ideas precisely.

Explanation of Mental Model:

This "poster style" mental model is designed for frequent viewing.

STEP SHEET

1. Study the mental model.
2. Write the definition of the word *angle* in your own words.
3. Compare your definition with a glossary definition.
4. Find additional words that are derived from the same word base(s).
5. Create a poster that illustrates the meaning of the word *angle*.

RUBRIC

Standard: Communication

Students will:
- Communicate their mathematical thinking coherently and clearly to peers, teachers, and others.
- Use the language of mathematics to express mathematical ideas precisely.

Criteria	4 Exceeds Standard	3 Meets Standard	2 Is Below Standard	1 Does Not Meet Standard
Mathematical language (1)	Writes definition that could be used as example for classroom	Writes accurate definition	Writes definition with minimal assistance	Cannot write definition with minimal assistance
Mathematical language (2)	Identifies numerous words that are derived from same word base(s)	Identifies at least three words that are derived from same word base(s)	Identifies words that are derived from same word base(s) with minimal assistance	Cannot identify words that are derived from same word base(s) with minimal assistance
Mental model	Designs mental model that could be used as example for classroom	Develops accurate personal mental model	Develops mental model with minimal assistance	Cannot design mental model with minimal assistance

The abscissa is the x-coordinate of a point on a coordinate graph. The abscissa of the point (3,5) is 3.

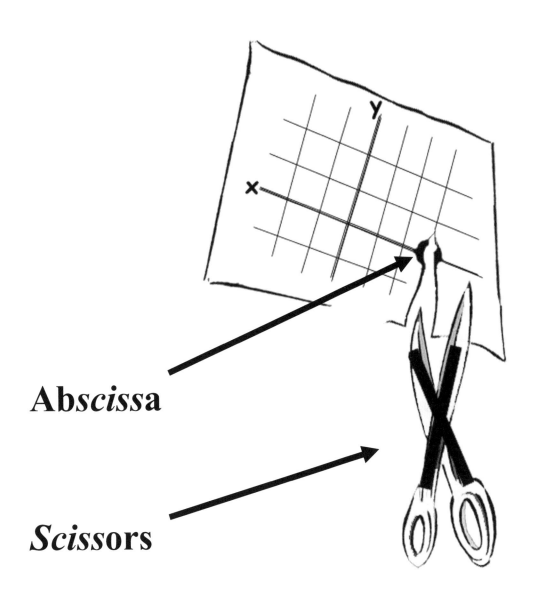

Abscissa

Scissors

The abscissa "tears" the x-axis into two pieces, just as scissors cut paper.

MENTAL MODEL—COMMUNICATION

Standard: Communication

Students will:
- Communicate their mathematical thinking coherently and clearly to peers, teachers, and others.
- Use the language of mathematics to express mathematical ideas precisely.

Explanation of Mental Model:

This "poster style" mental model is designed for frequent viewing.

STEP SHEET

1. Study the mental model.
2. Write a definition of the word *abscissa* in your own words.
3. Compare your definition with a dictionary definition.
4. Find additional words that are derived from the same word base(s).
5. Create a poster that illustrates the meaning of the word *abscissa*.

RUBRIC

Standard: Communication

Students will:
- Communicate their mathematical thinking coherently and clearly to peers, teachers, and others.
- Use the language of mathematics to express mathematical ideas precisely.

	4	3	2	1
Criteria	**Exceeds Standard**	**Meets Standard**	**Is Below Standard**	**Does Not Meet Standard**
Mathematical language (1)	Writes definition that becomes model for others	Writes accurate definition	Writes definition with minimal assistance	Cannot write definition with minimal assistance
Mathematical language (2)	Identifies numerous words that are derived from same word base(s)	Identifies at least three words that are derived from same word base(s)	Identifies words that are derived from same word base(s) with minimal assistance	Cannot identify words that are derived from same word base(s) with minimal assistance
Mental model	Designs mental model that could be used as example for classroom	Develops accurate personal mental model	Develops mental model with minimal assistance	Cannot design mental model with minimal assistance

Asymptote

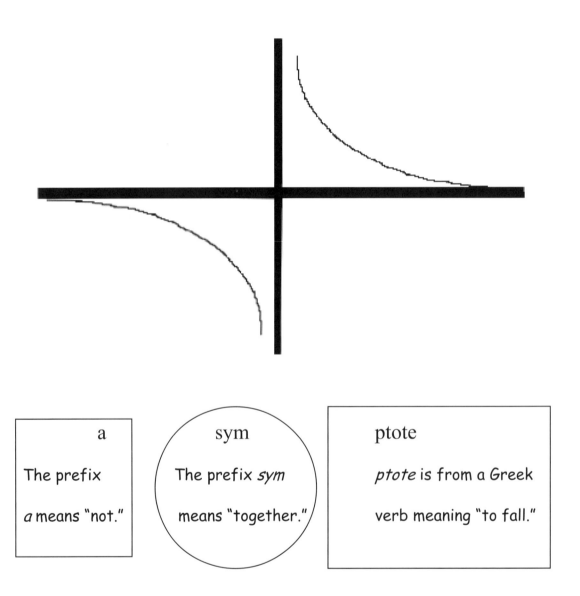

a	sym	ptote
The prefix *a* means "not."	The prefix *sym* means "together."	*ptote* is from a Greek verb meaning "to fall."

The word ***asymptote*** means "not falling together."

An asymptote is a line that does not "fall together" with another curve.

MENTAL MODEL—COMMUNICATION

Standard: Communication

Students will:
- Communicate their mathematical thinking coherently and clearly to peers, teachers, and others.
- Use the language of mathematics to express mathematical ideas precisely.

Explanation of Mental Model:

This "poster style" mental model is designed for frequent viewing.

STEP SHEET

1. Study the mental model.
2. Write a definition of the word *asymptote* in your own words.
3. Compare your definition with a dictionary definition.
4. Find additional words that are derived from the same base(s).
   For example:
   - The word *symptom* is a bodily condition that "falls together" with a disease.
   - A disease that does not reveal itself in bodily manifestations is said to be *asymptomatic*.
5. Create a poster that illustrates the meaning of the word *asymptote*.

RUBRIC

Standard: Communication

Students will:
- Communicate their mathematical thinking coherently and clearly to peers, teachers, and others.
- Use the language of mathematics to express mathematical ideas precisely.

Criteria	4 Exceeds Standard	3 Meets Standard	2 Is Below Standard	1 Does Not Meet Standard
Mathematical language (1)	Writes definition that becomes model for others	Writes accurate definition	Writes definition with minimal assistance	Cannot write definition with minimal assistance
Mathematical language (2)	Identifies numerous words that are derived from same word base(s)	Identifies at least three words that are derived from same word base(s)	Identifies words that are derived from same word base(s) with minimal assistance	Cannot identify words that are derived from same word base(s) with minimal assistance
Mental model	Designs a mental model that could be used as example for classroom	Develops accurate personal mental model	Develops mental model with minimal assistance	Cannot design mental model with minimal assistance

Lines

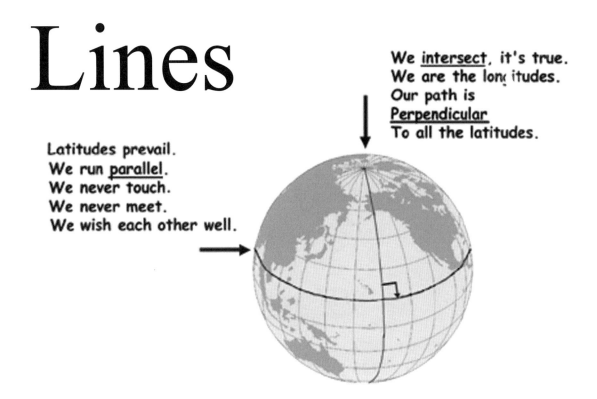

We <u>intersect</u>, it's true.
We are the longitudes.
Our path is
<u>Perpendicular</u>
To all the latitudes.

Latitudes prevail.
We run <u>parallel</u>.
We never touch.
We never meet.
We wish each other well.

Intersecting lines or line segments meet, or share, a common point. The point they share is called the point of intersection.

Two lines in the same plane that never intersect are called ***parallel lines***. If line 1 is parallel to line 2, we write this as

line 1 ∥ line 2.

Two lines that meet at a right angle are ***perpendicular***. If line 3 is perpendicular to line 4, we write this as

line 3 ⊥ line 4

MENTAL MODEL—CONNECTIONS

Standard: Connections

Recognize and apply mathematics in contexts outside mathematics.

Explanation of Mental Model:

This "poster style" mental model is designed for frequent viewing.

STEP SHEET

1. Study the mental model.
2. Write in your own words the definitions of the words *intersecting*, *parallel*, and *perpendicular*.
3. List at least three additional places that you find intersecting, parallel, and perpendicular lines.
4. Create a poster that illustrates parallel, perpendicular, and intersecting lines.

RUBRIC

Standard: Connections

Recognize and apply mathematics in contexts outside mathematics.

Criteria	4 Exceeds Standard	3 Meets Standard	2 Is Below Standard	1 Does Not Meet Standard
Mathematical language	Writes definition that could be used as example for classroom	Writes accurate definition	Writes definition with minimal assistance	Cannot write definition with minimal assistance
Problem solving	Identifies numerous places in environment that various lines can be found	Identifies at least five places in environment that various lines can be found	Identifies lines in environment with minimal assistance	Cannot identify lines in environment with minimal assistance
Mental model	Designs mental model that could be used as example for classroom	Develops accurate personal mental model	Develops mental model minimal assistance	Cannot design mental model with minimal assistance

APPENDIX

PLAN AND LABEL

MATH PROBLEM SOLVING

LETTER	WORD	SYMBOL	SENTENCE STARTER
E	Explore		I was asked to find …
P	Plan		I used …
S	Solve		I found …
E	Examine		The answer is … because …

Cannon County School District
Cannon County, Tennessee
2004–05 Secondary Math Teachers

www.ahaprocess.com

Plan and Label

Math Problem Solving

Letter	Step	Teacher Directions	Symbol	Sentence Starter
T	Task	Highlight math task		I am asked to …
I	Information	Circle important information		I knew …
P	Plan	Identify way to solve task		I will …
S	Solution	Show your work; choose your answer; write complete sentence with answer	Ⓐ Ⓑ Ⓒ Ⓓ	I found …

Caddo Parish School District
Shreveport, Louisiana
2004–05 Bethune Middle School
        Woodlawn High School

Plan and Label

Math Problem Solving

Letter	Step	Teacher Directions	Symbol	Sentence Starter
Q	Question	Use sentence frame to underline question		I was asked to …
T	Think	Thoughtfully, thoroughly, and totally read problem		
I	Information	Circle important information and labels; cross out unnecessary information	411	I knew …
P	Plan	Choose plan, operation, or strategy: OPERATION STRATEGY STEPS		I used …
S	Solution	Show your work; choose your answer; check your answer	X = 10	The answer is … because …

Lodi Unified Schools
Morada Middle School
Stockton, California
2004–05

Plan and Label in Math

1. 6⟌	Divisor: number of parts in a group
2. ⟌240	Dividend: total number of parts
3. 0⟌	Quotient: number of groups
4. 6⟌240	Are there enough parts for a group?
5. 6⟌240	Are there enough parts for a group? If so, how many groups?
6. ✗ 4 6⟌24 24	See if there are extra parts.

Writing Multiple-Choice Questions

Question:

a.

b.

c.

d.

Three rules:

1. One wrong-answer choice must be funny.

2. Only one answer choice can be right.

3. May not use "all of the above," "none of the above," etc.

Math Questions

1. Stems need to use the terminology.

2. Distracters are:

   - Incorrect operation

   - Incorrect order

   - Decimal in wrong place

   - Answer in wrong form (percentage instead of number, etc.)

   - Missed step

   - Unnecessary information included

   - Computational errors

CREDITS

CHAPTER ONE

Rational Numbers—Bethanie H. Tucker, Ed.D.
Practice for Mental Math—Source Unknown
Infinity Symbol—Bethanie H. Tucker, Ed.D.
Place Value—Bethanie H. Tucker, Ed.D.
Rounding—Bethanie H. Tucker, Ed.D.
Absolute Value (runners)—Bethanie H. Tucker, Ed.D.
Absolute Value (cars)—Shelley Rex
Ratio Ray—Bethanie H. Tucker, Ed.D.
Zero in Fractions—Bethanie H. Tucker, Ed.D.
Scientific Notation—Bethanie H. Tucker, Ed.D.
Matrices—Bethanie H. Tucker, Ed.D.
Algebra Tiles—Source Unknown
Window—Shelley Rex
Mr. FOIL—Source Unknown
Least Common Denominator—Shelley Rex
Greatest Common Factor—Shelley Rex
Story Mental Model (good guys, bad guys)—Source Unknown
Multiplying and Dividing Integers (triangle)—Shelley Rex
Addition and Subtraction of Integers (with two-color counters)—Shelley Rex

CHAPTER TWO

Dependent Variable—Bethanie H. Tucker, Ed.D.
Inequalities—Bethanie H. Tucker, Ed.D.
Proportionality—The Box—Shelley Rex (adapted from Alvin Independent
   School District math training materials)
Function (arrows)—Bethanie H. Tucker, Ed.D.
Vertical One-Touch Function Test—Bethanie H. Tucker, Ed.D.
Functions ("walked")—Shelley Rex
Interval Notation—Bethanie H. Tucker, Ed.D.
Crawl Before You Stand—Shelley Rex
Linear Equation (pirate map)—Bethanie H. Tucker, Ed.D.
Linear Equation (cartoon)—Bethanie H. Tucker, Ed.D.
Quadruplets—Bethanie H. Tucker, Ed.D.
Quadratic Equation—Bethanie H. Tucker, Ed.D.
Quadratic Formula—Bethanie H. Tucker, Ed.D.
Sloper-Size Machine—Bethanie H. Tucker, Ed.D.
Slope Formula—Bethanie H. Tucker, Ed.D.
Cups and Counters—Shelley Rex
Z-Box—Shelley Rex

CHAPTER THREE

Descartes in Bed—Bethanie H. Tucker, Ed.D.
Chords, Tangents, Diameter—Bethanie H. Tucker, Ed.D.
String Art—Bethanie H. Tucker, Ed.D.
Pythagorean Theorem: Elaboration on Pythagoras—Source Unknown
Pizza by the Sector—Bethanie H. Tucker, Ed.D.
Supplementary Vitamins—Bethanie H. Tucker, Ed.D.

CHAPTER FOUR

Area of Circle: Elaboration on Archimedes—Bethanie H. Tucker, Ed.D.
Area of Cylinder—Bethanie H. Tucker, Ed.D.
Cone—Bethanie H. Tucker, Ed.D.
Nautical Mile—Bethanie H. Tucker, Ed.D.
Gallon Guy—Source Unknown

CHAPTER FIVE

Order of Operations—Bethanie H. Tucker, Ed.D.
QDPAC—adapted from Addison-Wesley math
D=RT—Bethanie H. Tucker, Ed.D.
Problem-Solving Process—Judy Sain

CHAPTER SIX

Box and Whisker Plot— Bethanie H. Tucker, Ed.D.
Probability—Source Unknown
Conjectures—Bethanie H. Tucker, Ed.D.
Angle—Bethanie H. Tucker, Ed.D.
Abscissa—Bethanie H. Tucker, Ed.D.
Asymptote—Bethanie H. Tucker, Ed.D.
Lines—Bethanie H. Tucker, Ed.D.

www.ahaprocess.com
PO Box 727, Highlands, TX 77562-0727
(800) 424-9484; fax: (281) 426-8705
store@ahaprocess.com

ORDER FORM

UPS SHIP TO ADDRESS (no post office boxes, please):

NAME: _____ E-mail _____ PHONE: _____

ORGANIZATION: _____

ADDRESS: _____ CITY _____

STATE/ZIP: _____ FAX: _____

QTY	TITLE	1-4 Copies	5+ Copies *	Total
	A Framework for Understanding Poverty	22.00	15.00	
	A Framework for Understanding Poverty workbook	7.00	7.00	
	Understanding Learning	7.00	7.00	
	Learning Structures workbook (always comes with *Understanding Learning*)	10.00	10.00	
	A Framework for Understanding Poverty audio workshop Kit (includes Day 1 & 2, 8 CDs—and 4 books listed above) **S/H: $10.50**	295.00	295.00	
	A Framework for Understanding Poverty audio book (3-CD set includes book)	35.00	35.00	
	Un Marco Para Entender La Pobreza (*Framework* translated into Spanish)	22.00	15.00	
	Putting the Pieces Together workbook (replaces *Application of Learning Structures*)	10.00	10.00	
	A Picture Is Worth a Thousand Words	18.00	15.00	
	Berrytales—Plays in One Act	25.00	20.00	
	Bridges Out of Poverty: Strategies for Professionals and Communities	22.00	15.00	
	Bridges Out of Poverty audio book (7-CD set/includes book)	40.00	40.00	
	Bridges Out of Poverty overview (recording of online e-learning) DVD *	15.00	15.00	
	Changing Children's Minds	30.00	30.00	
	Crossing the Tracks for Love	14.95	14.95	
	Crossing the Tracks for Love audio book (4-CD set with book)	30.00	30.00	
	Daily Math Practice for Virginia SOLs—Grade 4	22.00	15.00	
	Daily Math Skills Review Grade 4—practice for mastery of math standards	22.00	15.00	
	Getting Ahead in a Just-Gettin'-By World and *Facilitator Notes* (set)	25.00	25.00	
	Getting Ahead in a Just-Gettin'-By World (after purchasing a set)	15.00	15.00	
	Getting Ahead … Facilitator Notes (after purchasing a set)	10.00	10.00	
	Hear Our Cry: Boys in Crisis	22.00	15.00	
	Hidden Rules of Class at Work	22.00	15.00	
	Living on a Tightrope: a Survival Handbook for Principals	22.00	15.00	
	Mental Models for Math	10.00	10.00	
	Mr. Base Ten Invents Math	22.00	15.00	
	Parenting Someone Else's Child: The Foster Parents' 'How-To' Manual	22.00	15.00	
	Removing the Mask: Giftedness in Poverty	25.00	20.00	
	Environmental Opportunity Profile (EOP set/includes 1 FAQ)	25.00	25.00	
	Additional FAQs, EOPs	3.00	3.00	
	Slocumb-Payne Teacher Perception Inventory (TPI 25/set)	25.00	25.00	
	Using Your Own Campus Norms to Identify Gifted Students—DVD *	15.00	15.00	
	Gifted combo: 1 set each EOP, TPI, FAQ, Using Your Campus Norms DVD *	58.00	58.00	
	The Journey of Al and Gebra to the Land of Algebra	18.00	15.00	
	Think Rather of Zebra: Dealing with Aspects of Poverty Through Story	18.00	15.00	
	Trainer's Companion: Stories to Stimulate Reflection, Conversation, Action	22.00	15.00	
	What Every Church Member Should Know About Poverty	22.00	15.00	
	What Every Church Member Should Know …—3 sermons on audiotape	25.00	25.00	
	Working With Parents Building Relationship for Student Success	5.00	5.00	
	Working with Students: Discipline Strategies for the Classroom	10.00	10.00	
	Jodi's Stories – A Companion Piece to Bridges Out of Poverty DVD **S/H: $4.50**	150.00	150.00	
	Tucker Signing Strategies for Reading video and manual **S/H: $8.50**	195.00	195.00	
	Tucker Signing Strategies Just for Kids! (recording of online e-learning) DVD *	30.00	30.00	
	Tucker Signs reference cards on CD	25.00	25.00	
	Take-Home Books for Tucker Signing Strategies for Reading	22.00	15.00	
	Grammar Graphics Program **S/H: $8.50**	129.00	129.00	
	Preventing School Violence—5 videos and manual **S/H: $15.00**	995.00	995.00	
	Preventing School Violence CD—PowerPoint presentation	25.00	25.00	
	Preventing School Violence by Creating Emotional Safety training manual	15.00	15.00	
	Meeting Standards & Raising Test Scores—When You Don't Have Much Time or Money (4 videos/training manual). Specify VHS or DVD **S/H: $15.00**	995.00	995.00	
	Meeting Standards & Raising Test Scores Training manual	18.00	18.00	
	Meeting Standards & Raising Test Scores Resource manual	18.00	18.00	
	Rita's Stories (2 VHS videos) **S/H: $8.50** Rita's Stories DVD **S/H: $4.50**	150.00	150.00	
	Ruby Payne video sampler (specify VHS or DVD) **S/H: $4.50**	10.00	10.00	
	aha! Process 12-oz. mugs (white with red logo and website)	8.00	2 @15.00	
	Walk-Through Rubric Notepads—**Circle one:** General; Mutual Respect; Instruction; Discipline & Classroom Management; Audit for Differentiated Instruction; Assorted	5 @5.00	50 @30.00	

For Certified Trainers only—Please note date/city of training:

	A Framework for Understanding Poverty video sets (12 modules) (Day 1 & Day 2 of *Framework* seminar) Circle one: VHS or DVD **S/H: $25.00**	1995.00	1995.00	
	Single Framework DVD # _____, _____, _____	225.00	225.00	
	A Framework for Understanding Poverty CD—PowerPoint presentation	50.00	50.00	
	A Framework for Understanding Poverty CD—Enhanced PowerPoint presentation	100.00	100.00	
	Meeting Standards & Raising Test Scores CD—PowerPoint presentation	50.00	50.00	
	Bridges Out of Poverty CD—PowerPoint presentation	50.00	50.00	
	Bridges Out of Poverty DVD Series (7 modules) **S/H $8.50**	695.00	695.00	
	Single Bridges DVD # ____, ____, ____	150.00	150.00	

Total Quantity	
Subtotal	
S/H	
Tax	
Total	

TERMS: S/H: 1-4 books—$4.50 plus $2.00 each additional book up to 4 books (1 calendar $2)
5+ books—8% of total (special S/H for videos). E-mail (see top right) for international rates.
TAX: Rate determined by location of sale.
Prices subject to change. Visit aha! Process website (www.ahaprocess.com) for current offerings.

AmEx   MC   Visa   Discover

CREDIT CARD # _____ EXP. DATE _____ Signature _____
AUTHORIZATION # _____ PO # _____ (please fax PO with order) Check # _____.

* Orders placed by participants while attending U.S. National Tour or Trainer Certification receive quantity (5 or more) pricing.

More eye-openers at ...

www.ahaprocess.com

Interested in more information?

We invite you to our website, www.ahaprocess.com, to join our **aha!** News List!

Receive the latest income and poverty statistics free when you join! Then receive **aha!** News, along with periodic updates!

Also on the website:
- Success stories from our participants—from schools, social services, and businesses
- Complete listing of aha! workshops and trainer certification programs
- Read the latest aha! School Reform Research
- Learn more about the Payne Reform Model
- See an up-to-date listing of our books and videos
- Shop at our convenient online store
- Register for Dr. Ruby Payne's U.S. National Tour
- Watch a videoclip of Dr. Payne
- Look at news articles from around the country

And more ...